Hands-On Deep Learning with Go

with Go

A practical guide to building and implementing neural network models using Go

Gareth Seneque
Darrell Chua

BIRMINGHAM - MUMBAI

Hands-On Deep Learning with Go

Copyright © 2019 Packt Publishing

Commissioning Editor: Pravin Dhandre
Acquisition Editor: Joshua Nadar
Content Development Editor: Roshan Kumar
Senior Editor: Jack Cummings
Technical Editor: Dinesh Chaudhary
Copy Editor: Safis Editing
Project Coordinator: Namrata Swetta
Proofreader: Safis Editing
Indexer: Manju Arasan
Production Designer: Jayalaxmi Raja

First published: August 2019

Production reference: 1060819

Published by Packt Publishing Ltd.
Livery Place
35 Livery Street
Birmingham
B3 2PB, UK.

ISBN 978-1-78934-099-0

www.packtpub.com

Contributors

About the authors

Gareth Seneque is a machine learning engineer with 11 years' experience of building and deploying systems at scale in the finance and media industries. He became interested in deep learning in 2014 and is currently building a search platform within his organization, using neuro-linguistic programming and other machine learning techniques to generate content metadata and drive recommendations. He has contributed to a number of open source projects, including CoREBench and Gorgonia. He also has extensive experience with modern DevOps practices, using AWS, Docker, and Kubernetes to effectively distribute the processing of machine learning workloads.

Darrell Chua is a senior data scientist with more than 10 years' experience. He has developed models of varying complexity, from building credit scorecards with logistic regression to creating image classification models for trading cards. He has spent the majority of his time working with in fintech companies, trying to bring machine learning technologies into the world of finance. He has been programming in Go for several years and has been working on deep learning models for even longer. Among his achievements is the creation of numerous business intelligence and data science pipelines that enable the delivery of a top-of-the-line automated underwriting system, producing near-instant approval decisions.

About the reviewer

Xuanyi Chew is the primary author of Gorgonia. In his day job, he is the chief data scientist of a rapidly growing local start-up in Sydney. At night, he works on his hobbies of building deep learning AI (using Gorgonia), furthering his hopes of one day building an AGI. He wants to make Go the primary ecosystem for machine learning work and would love your help.

Packt is searching for authors like you

If you're interested in becoming an author for Packt, please visit `authors.packtpub.com` and apply today. We have worked with thousands of developers and tech professionals, just like you, to help them share their insight with the global tech community. You can make a general application, apply for a specific hot topic that we are recruiting an author for, or submit your own idea.

Table of Contents

Preface

Go is an open source programming language designed by Google to handle huge projects efficiently. It makes building reliable, simple, and efficient software straightforward and easy.

This book immediately jumps into the practicalities of implementing **Deep Neural Networks** (**DNNs**) in Go. Simply put, the book's title contains its aim. This means there will be a lot of technical detail, a lot of code, and (not too much) math. By the time you finally close the book or turn off your Kindle, you'll know how (and why) to implement modern, scalable DNNs, and be able to repurpose them for your needs in whatever industry or mad science project you're involved.

Who this book is for

This book is for data scientists, machine learning engineers, and deep learning aspirants who are looking to inject deep learning into their Go applications. Familiarity with machine learning and basic Golang code is expected in order to get the most out of this book.

What this book covers

Chapter 1, *Introduction to Deep Learning in Go*, introduces the history and applications of deep learning. This chapter also gives an overview of ML with Go.

Chapter 2, *What is a Neural Network and How Do I Train One?*, covers how to build a simple neural network and how to inspect a graph, as well as many of the commonly used activation functions. This chapter also discusses some of the different options for gradient descent algorithms and optimizations for your neural network.

Chapter 3, *Beyond Basic Neural Networks – Autoencoders and RBMs*, shows how to build a simple multilayer neural network and an autoencoder. This chapter also explores the design and implementation of a probabilistic graphical model, an RBM, used in an unsupervised manner to create a recommendation engine for films.

Chapter 4, *CUDA – GPU-Accelerated Training*, looks at the hardware side of deep learning and also at exactly how CPUs and GPUs serve our computational needs.

Chapter 5, *Next Word Prediction with Recurrent Neural Networks*, goes into what a basic RNN is and how to train one. You will also get a clear idea of the RNN architecture, including GRU/LSTM networks.

Chapter 6, *Object Recognition with Convolutional Neural Networks*, shows you how to build a CNN and how to tune some of the hyperparameters (such as the number of epochs and batch sizes) in order to get the desired result and get it running smoothly on different computers.

Chapter 7, *Maze Solving with Deep Q-Networks*, gives an introduction to reinforcement learning and Q-learning and how to build a DQN and solve a maze.

Chapter 8, *Generative Models with Variational Autoencoders*, shows how to build a VAE and looks at the advantages of a VAE over a standard autoencoder. This chapter also shows how to understand the effect of varying latent space dimensions on a network.

Chapter 9, *Building a Deep Learning Pipeline*, looks at what data pipelines are and why we use Pachyderm to build or manage them.

Chapter 10, *Scaling Deployment*, looks at a number of the technologies that sit underneath Pachyderm, including Docker and Kubernetes, and also examines how we can deploy stacks to cloud infrastructure using these tools .

To get the most out of this book

This book primarily uses Go, the Gorgonia package for Go, the Cu package for Go, CUDA (plus drivers) from NVIDIA, and an NVIDIA GPU that supports CUDA. Docker is also needed for Section 3, *Pipeline, Deployment, and Beyond!*

Download the example code files

You can download the example code files for this book from your account at www.packt.com. If you purchased this book elsewhere, you can visit www.packt.com/support and register to have the files emailed directly to you.

You can download the code files by following these steps:

1. Log in or register at www.packt.com.
2. Select the **SUPPORT** tab.
3. Click on **Code Downloads & Errata**.
4. Enter the name of the book in the **Search** box and follow the onscreen instructions.

Once the file is downloaded, please make sure that you unzip or extract the folder using the latest version of:

- WinRAR/7-Zip for Windows
- Zipeg/iZip/UnRarX for Mac
- 7-Zip/PeaZip for Linux

The code bundle for the book is also hosted on GitHub at https://github.com/ PacktPublishing/Hands-On-Deep-Learning-with-Go. In case there's an update to the code, it will be updated on the existing GitHub repository.

We also have other code bundles from our rich catalog of books and videos available at https://github.com/PacktPublishing/Hands-On-Deep-Learning-with-Go. Check them out!

Download the color images

We also provide a PDF file that has color images of the screenshots/diagrams used in this book. You can download it here: http://www.packtpub.com/sites/default/files/ downloads/9781789340990_ColorImages.pdf.

Conventions used

There are a number of text conventions used throughout this book.

CodeInText: Indicates code words in text, database table names, folder names, filenames, file extensions, pathnames, dummy URLs, user input, and Twitter handles. Here is an example: "Mount the downloaded WebStorm-10*.dmg disk image file as another disk in your system."

A block of code is set as follows:

```
type nn struct {
    g *ExprGraph
    w0, w1 *Node

    pred *Node
}
```

When we wish to draw your attention to a particular part of a code block, the relevant lines or items are set in bold:

```
intercept Ctrl+C
    sigChan := make(chan os.Signal, 1)
    signal.Notify(sigChan, syscall.SIGINT, syscall.SIGTERM)
    doneChan := make(chan bool, 1)
```

Any command-line input or output is written as follows:

```
sudo apt install nvidia-390 nvidia-cuda-toolkit libcupti-dev
```

Bold: Indicates a new term, an important word, or words that you see on screen. For example, words in menus or dialog boxes appear in the text like this. Here is an example: "Select **System info** from the **Administration** panel."

Warnings or important notes appear like this.

Tips and tricks appear like this.

Get in touch

Feedback from our readers is always welcome.

General feedback: If you have questions about any aspect of this book, mention the book title in the subject of your message and email us at customercare@packtpub.com.

Errata: Although we have taken every care to ensure the accuracy of our content, mistakes do happen. If you have found a mistake in this book, we would be grateful if you would report this to us. Please visit www.packt.com/submit-errata, selecting your book, clicking on the Errata Submission Form link, and entering the details.

Piracy: If you come across any illegal copies of our works in any form on the Internet, we would be grateful if you would provide us with the location address or website name. Please contact us at copyright@packt.com with a link to the material.

If you are interested in becoming an author: If there is a topic that you have expertise in and you are interested in either writing or contributing to a book, please visit authors.packtpub.com.

Reviews

Please leave a review. Once you have read and used this book, why not leave a review on the site that you purchased it from? Potential readers can then see and use your unbiased opinion to make purchase decisions, we at Packt can understand what you think about our products, and our authors can see your feedback on their book. Thank you!

For more information about Packt, please visit packt.com.

Section 1: Deep Learning in Go, Neural Networks, and How to Train Them

This section introduces you to **deep learning** (DL) and the libraries in Go that are needed to design, implement, and train **deep neural networks** (DNNs). We also cover the implementation of an autoencoder for unsupervised learning, and a **restricted Boltzmann machine** (RBM) for a Netflix-style collaborative filtering system.

The following chapters are included in this section:

- Chapter 1, *Introduction to Deep Learning in Go*
- Chapter 2, *What is a Neural Network and How Do I Train One?*
- Chapter 3, *Beyond Basic Neural Networks - Autoencoders and Restricted Boltzmann Machines*
- Chapter 4, *CUDA - GPU-Accelerated Training*

Introduction to Deep Learning in Go

This book will very quickly jump into the practicalities of implementing **Deep Neural Networks** (**DNNs**) in Go. Simply put, this book's title contains its aim. This means there will be a lot of technical detail, a lot of code, and (not too much) math. By the time you finally close this book or turn off your Kindle, you'll know how (and why) to implement modern, scalable DNNs and be able to repurpose them for your needs in whatever industry or mad science project you're involved in.

Our choice of Go reflects the maturing of the landscape of Go libraries built for the kinds of operations our DNNs perform. There is, of course, much debate about the trade-offs made when selecting languages or libraries, and we will devote a section of this chapter to our views and argue for the choices we've made.

However, what is code without context? Why do we care about this seemingly convoluted mix of linear algebra, calculus, statistics, and probability? Why use computers to recognize things in images or identify aberrant patterns in financial data? And, perhaps most importantly, what do the approaches to these tasks have in common? The initial sections of this book will try to provide some of this context.

Scientific endeavor, when broken up into the disciplines that represent their institutional and industry specialization, is governed by an idea of progress. By this, we mean a kind of momentum, a moving forward, toward some end. For example, the ideal goal of medicine is to be able to identify and cure any ailment or disease. Physicists aim to understand completely the fundamental laws of nature. Progress trends in this general direction. Science is itself an optimization method. So, what might the ultimate goal of **Machine Learning** (**ML**) be?

We'll be upfront. We think it's the creation of **Artificial General Intelligence (AGI)**. That's the prize: a general-purpose learning computer to take care of the jobs and leave life to people. As we will see when we cover the history of **Deep Learning (DL)** in detail, founders of the top **Artificial Intelligence (AI)** labs agree that AGI represents a *meta-solution* to many of the complex problems in our world today, from economics to medicine to government.

This chapter will cover the following topics:

- Why DL?
- DL—history applications
- Overview of ML in Go
- Using Gorgonia

Introducing DL

We will now offer a high-level view of why DL is important and how it fits into the discussion about AI. Then, we will look at the historical development of DL, as well as current and future applications.

Why DL?

So, who are you, dear reader? Why are you interested in DL? Do you have your private vision for AI? Or do you have something more modest? What is your *origin story*?

In our survey of colleagues, teachers, and meetup acquaintances, the origin story of someone with a more formal interest in machines has a few common features. It doesn't matter much if you grew up playing games against the computer, an invisible enemy who sometimes glitched out, or if you chased down actual bots in *id Software's Quake* back in the late 1990s; the idea of some combination of software and hardware thinking and acting independently had an impact on each of us early on in life.

And then, as time passed, with age, education, and exposure to pop culture, your ideas grew refined and maybe you ended up as a researcher, engineer, hacker, or hobbyist, and now you're wondering how you might participate in booting up the grand machine.

If your interests are more modest, say you are a data scientist looking to understand cutting-edge techniques, but are ambivalent about all of this talk of sentient software and science fiction, you are, in many ways, better prepared for the realities of ML in 2019 than most. Each of us, regardless of the scale of our ambition, must understand the logic of code and hard work through trial and error. Thankfully, we have very fast graphics cards.

And what is the result of these basic truths? Right now, in 2019, DL has had an impact on our lives in numerous ways. Hard problems are being solved. Some trivial, some not. Yes, Netflix has a model of your most embarrassing movie preferences, but Facebook has automatic image annotation for the visually impaired. Understanding the potential impact of DL is as simple as watching the expression of joy on the face of someone who has just seen a photo of a loved one for the first time.

DL – a history

We will now briefly cover the history of DL and the historical context from which it emerged, including the following:

- The idea of **AI**
- The beginnings of computer science/information theory
- Current academic work about the state/future of DL systems

While we are specifically interested in DL, the field didn't emerge out of nothing. It is a group of models/algorithms within ML itself, a branch of computer science. It forms one approach to AI. The other, so-called **symbolic AI**, revolves around hand-crafted (rather than learned) features and rules written in code, rather than a weighted model that contains patterns extracted from data algorithmically.

The idea of thinking machines, before becoming a science, was very much a fiction that began in antiquity. The Greek god of arms manufacturing, *Hephaestus*, built automatons out of gold and silver. They served his whims and are an early example of human imagination naturally considering what it might take to replicate an embodied form of itself.

Bringing the history forward a few thousand years, there are several key figures in 20th-century information theory and computer science that built the platform that allowed the development of AI as a distinct field, including the recent work in DL we will be covering.

The first major figure, Claude Shannon, offered us a general theory of communication. Specifically, he described, in his landmark paper, *A Mathematical Theory of Computation*, how to ensure against information loss when transmitting over an imperfect medium (like, say, using vacuum tubes to perform computation). This notion, particularly his noisy-channel coding theorem, proved crucial for handling arbitrarily large quantities of data and algorithms reliably, without the errors of the medium itself being introduced into the communications channel.

Alan Turing described his *Turing machine* in 1936, offering us a universal model of computation. With the fundamental building blocks he described, he defined the limits of what a machine might compute. He was influenced by John Von Neumann's idea of the *stored-program*. The key insight from Turing's work is that digital computers can simulate any process of formal reasoning (the *Church-Turing* hypothesis). The following diagram shows the Turing machine process:

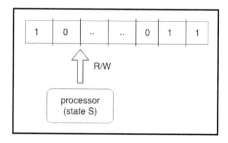

So, you mean to tell us, Mr. Turing, that computers might be made to reason...like us?!

John Von Neumann was himself influenced by Turing's 1936 paper. Before the development of the transistor, when vacuum tubes were the only means of computation available (in systems such as ENIAC and its derivatives), John Von Neumann published his final work. It remained incomplete at his death and is entitled *The Computer and the Brain*. Despite remaining incomplete, it gave early consideration to how models of computation may operate in the brain as they do in machines, including observations from early neuroscience around the connections between neurons and synapses.

Since AI was first conceived as a discrete field of research in 1956, with ML coined in 1959, the field has gone through a much-discussed ebb and flow—periods where hype and funding were plentiful, and periods where private sector money was non-existent and research conferences wouldn't even accept papers that emphasized neural network approaches to building AI systems.

Within AI itself, these competing approaches cannibalized research dollars and talent. Symbolic AI met its limitations in the sheer impossibility of handcrafting rules for advanced tasks such as image classification, speech recognition, and machine translation. ML sought to radically reconfigure this process. Instead of applying a bunch of human-written rules to data and hoping to get answers, human labor was, instead, to be spent on building a machine that could infer rules from data when the answers were known. This is an example of *supervised learning*, where the machine learns an essential *cat-ness* after processing thousands of example images with an associated *cat* label.

Quite simply, the idea was to have a system that could generalize. After all, the goal is AGI. Take a picture of your family's newest furry feline and the computer, using its understanding of *cat-ness*, correctly identifies a *cat*! An active area of research within ML, one thought essential for building a general AI, is *transfer learning*, where we might take the machine that understands *cat-ness* and plug it into a machine that, in turn, acts when *cat-ness* is identified. This is the approach many AI labs around the world are taking: building systems out of systems, augmenting algorithmic weakness in one area with statistical near certainty in another, and, hopefully, building a system that better serves human (or business) needs.

The notion of *serving human needs* brings us to an important point regarding the ethics of AI (and the DL approaches we will be looking at). There has been much discussion in the media and academic or industry circles around the ethical implications of these systems. What does it mean for our society if we have easy, automated, widespread surveillance thanks to advances in computer vision? What about automated weapons systems or manufacturing? It is no longer a stretch to imagine vast warehouses staffed by nothing with a pulse. What then for the people who used to do those jobs?

Of course, full consideration of these important issues lies outside the scope of this book, but this is the context in which our work takes place. You will be one of the privileged few able to build these systems and move the field forward. The work of the **Future of Humanity Institute** at Oxford University, run by Nick Bostrom, and the **Future of Life Institute**, run by MIT physicist, Max Tegmark, are two examples of where the kind of academic debate around AI ethics issues is taking place. This debate is not limited to academic or non-profit circles, however; DeepMind, an Alphabet company whose goal is to be an *Apollo program for AGI*, launched *DeepMind Ethics & Society* in October 2017.

This may seem far removed from the world of code and CUDA and neural networks to recognize cat pictures, but, as progress is made and these systems become more advanced and have more wide-ranging applications, our societies will face real consequences. As researchers and developers, it behooves us to have some answers, or at least ideas of how we might deal with these challenges when we have to face them.

DL – hype or breakthrough?

DL and the associated hype is a relatively recent development. Most discussion of its *emergence* centers around the ImageNet benchmarks of 2012, where a deep convolutional neural network beat the previous year's error rate by 9%, a significant improvement where previous winners had made incremental improvements at best with techniques that used hand-crafted features in their models. The following diagram shows this improvement:

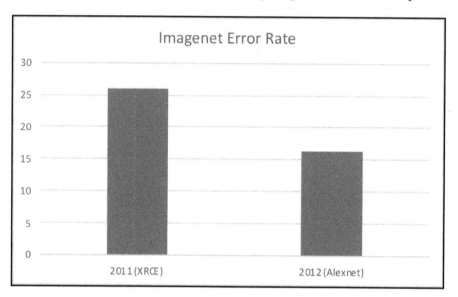

Despite the recent hype, the components that make DL work, which allow us to train deep models, have proven very effective in image classification and various other tasks. These were developed in the 1980s by Geoffrey Hinton and his group at the University of Toronto. Their early work took place during one of the *flow* periods discussed earlier in this chapter. Indeed, they were wholly dependent on funding from the **Canadian Institute for Advanced Research (CIFAR)**.

As the 21st century began in earnest, after the tech bubble that had burst in March 2000 began to inflate again, the availability of high-performance GPUs and the growth in computational power more generally meant that these techniques, which had been developed decades earlier but had gone unused due to a lack of funding and industry interest, suddenly became viable. Benchmarks that previously saw only incremental improvements in image recognition, speech recognition, natural language processing, and sequence modeling all had their *y*-axes adjusted.

It was not just massive advances in hardware paired with old algorithms that got us to this point. There have been algorithmic advances that have allowed us to train particularly deep networks. The most well-known of these is batch normalization, introduced in 2015. It ensures numeric stabilization across layers and can prevent exploding gradients, reducing training time dramatically. There is still active debate about *why* batch normalization is so effective. An example of this is a paper published in May 2018 refuting the central premise of the original paper, namely, that it is not the *internal co-variant shift* that is reduced, rather it *makes the optimization landscape smoother*, that is, the gradients can more reliably propagate, and the effects of a learning rate on training time and stability are more predictable.

Collectively, from the folk science of ancient Greek myths to the very real breakthroughs in information theory, neuroscience, and computer science, specifically in models of computation, have combined to produce network architectures and the algorithms needed to train them that scale well to solving many fundamental AI tasks in 2018 that had proven intractable for decades.

Defining deep learning

Now, let's take a step back and start with a simple, working definition of DL. As we work through this book, our understanding of this term will evolve, but, for now, let's consider a simple example. We have an image of a person. How can we *show* this image to a computer? How can we *teach* the computer to associate this image with the word *person*?

First, we figure out a representation of this image, say the RGB values for every pixel in the image. We then feed that array of values (together with several trainable parameters) into a series of operations we're quite familiar with (multiplication and addition). This produces a new representation that we can use to compare against a representation we know maps to the label, *person*. We automate this process of comparison and update the values of our parameters as we go.

This description covers a simple, shallow ML system. We'll get into more detail in a later chapter devoted to neural networks but, for now, to make this system deep, we increase the number of operations on a greater number of parameters. This allows us to capture more information regarding the thing we're representing (the person's image). The biological model that influences the design of this system is the human nervous system, including neurons (the things we fill with our representations) and synapses (the trainable parameters).

The following diagram shows the ML system in progress:

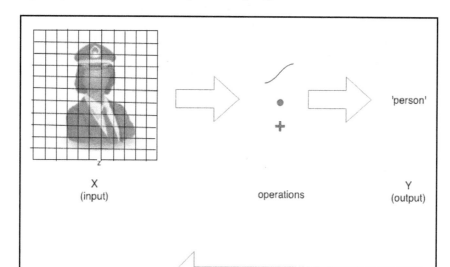

So, DL is just an evolutionary twist on the 1957's *perceptron*, the simplest and the original binary classifier. This twist, together with dramatic increases in computing power, is the difference between a system that doesn't work and a system that allows a car to drive autonomously.

Beyond self-driving cars, there are numerous applications for DL and related approaches in farming, crop management, and satellite image analysis. Advanced computer vision powers machines that remove weeds and reduce pesticide use. We have near-real-time voice search that is fast and accurate. This is the fundamental stuff of society, from food production to communication. Additionally, we are also on the cusp of compelling, real-time video and audio generation, which will make today's privacy debates or drama about what is *fake news* look minor.

Long before we get to AGI, we can improve the world around us using the discoveries we make along the way. DL is one of these discoveries. It will drive an increase in automation, which, as long as the political change that accompanies it is supportive, can offer improvements across any number of industries, meaning goods and services will get cheaper, faster, and more widely available. Ideally, this means people will be set increasingly free from the routines of their ancestors.

The darker side of progress is not to be forgotten either. Machine vision that can identify victims can also identify targets. Indeed, the Future of Life Institute's open letter on autonomous weapons (*Autonomous Weapons: an Open Letter from AI & Robotics Researchers*), endorsed by science and tech luminaries such as Stephen Hawking and Elon Musk, is an example of the interplay and tensions between academic departments, industry labs, and governments about what the right kind of progress is. In our world, the nation-state has traditionally controlled the guns and the money. Advanced AI can be weaponized, and this is a race where perhaps one group wins and the rest of us lose.

More concretely, the field of ML is progressing incredibly fast. How might we measure this? The premier ML conference **Neural Information Processing Systems** (**NIPS**) has over seven times the registrations in the year 2017 that it did in 2010.

Registrations for 2018 happened more in the manner of a rock concert than a dry technical conference, reflected in the following statistic tweeted out by the organizers themselves:

The *de facto* central repository of ML preprints, **arXiv**, has a hockey-stick growth chart of such extremes, where tools have emerged to help researchers to track all of the new work. An example of this is the director of AI at Tesla, Andrej Karpathy's site, arxiv-sanity (http://www.arxiv-sanity.com/). This site allows us to sort/group papers and organize an interface by which we can pull research we're interested in from the stream of publications with relative ease.

We cannot predict what will happen to the rate of progress over the next five years. The professional guesses of venture capitalists and pundits range from exponential to *the next AI winter is nigh*. But we have techniques and libraries and compute power *now,* and knowing how to use them at their limits for a natural language processing or computer vision task can help to solve real-world problems.

This is what our book aims to show you how to do.

Overview of ML in Go

This section will take a look at the ML ecosystem in Go, first discussing the essentials we want from a library, and then assessing each of the main Go ML libraries in turn.

Go's ML ecosystem has historically been quite limited. The language was introduced in 2009, well before the DL revolution that has brought many new programmers into the fold. You might assume that Go has seen the growth in libraries and tools that other languages have. History, instead, determined that many of the higher-level APIs for the mathematical operations that underpin our networks have appeared as Python libraries (or have complete Python bindings). There are numerous well-known examples of this, including PyTorch, Keras, TensorFlow, Theano, and Caffe (you get the idea).

Unfortunately, these libraries have either zero or incomplete bindings for Go. For example, TensorFlow can do inference (*Is this a cat or not?*), but not training (*What is a cat anyway? Oh, okay, I'll take a look at these examples and figure it out*). While this takes advantage of Go's strengths when it comes to deployment (compilation down to single binary, compiler speed, and low memory footprint), from a developer's perspective, you're then forced to work across two languages (Python for training your model and Go for running it).

Issues you may face, beyond the cognitive hit of switching syntax when designing, implementing, or troubleshooting, extend to environment and configuration problems. These problems include questions such as: *Is my Go environment configured properly? Is my Python 2 binary symlinked to Python or is it Python 3? Is TensorFlow GPU working properly?* If our interest is in designing the best model and getting it trained and deployed in the minimum amount of time, none of the Python or Go bindings libraries are suitable.

It is important, at this point, to ask: so, what do we want out of a *DL library* in Go? Quite simply, we want as much unnecessary complication abstracted away as possible while preserving flexibility and control over our model and how it is trained.

What does this mean in practice? The following list outlines the answers to this query:

- We do not want to interface with **Basic Linear Algebra Subprograms** (**BLAS**) directly to construct basic operations such as multiplication and addition.
- We do not want to define a tensor type and associated function(s) each time we implement a new network.
- We do not want to write an implementation of **Stochastic Gradient Descent** (**SGD**) from scratch each time we want to train our network.

The following are some of the things that will be covered in this book:

- **Automatic or symbolic differentiation**: Our DNN is trying to learn some function. It iteratively *solves* the problem of *what is the function that will take an input image and output the label cat?* by calculating the gradient (the *gradient descent optimizations*) with respect to the loss (*how wrong is our function?*). This allows us to understand whether to change the weights in our network and by how much, with the specific mode of differentiation *breaking up* the calculation of these gradients (effectively using the chain rule), giving us the performance we need to be able to train deep networks with millions of parameters.

- **Numerical stabilization functions**: This is essential for DL, as we will explore in later sections of this book. A primary example of this is **Batch Normalization** or BatchNorm, as the attendant function is often called. It aims to put our data on the same scale to increase training speed, and it reduces the possibility of maximum values cascading through the layers and causing gradient explosion (something we will discuss in greater detail in Chapter 2, *What is a Neural Network and How Do I Train One?*).

- **Activation functions**: These are mathematical operations that introduce nonlinearities into the various layers in our neural network and help to determine which neurons in a layer will be *activated*, passing their values down to the next layer in the network. Examples include Sigmoid, **Rectified Linear Unit (ReLU)**, and Softmax. These will be considered in greater detail in Chapter 2, *What is a Neural Network and How Do I Train One?*

- **Gradient descent optimizations**: We will also cover these extensively in Chapter 2, *What is a Neural Network and How Do I Train One?* But, as the primary optimization method used in DNNs, we consider this a core function necessary for any library to have DL as its purpose.

- **CUDA support**: Nvidia's drivers allow us to offload the fundamental operations involved in our DNNs to our GPU. GPUs are really great for parallel workloads involving matrix transformations (indeed, this was their original purpose: computing the world-geometry of games) and can reduce the time it takes to train your model by an order of magnitude or more. Suffice to say, CUDA support is essential for modern DNN implementations and is therefore available in the major Python libraries described previously.

- **Deployment tools**: As we will cover in `Chapter 9`, *Building a Deep Learning Pipeline*, deployment of a model for training or inference is often overlooked in discussions about DL. With neural network architectures growing more complex, and with the availability of vast amounts of data, training your network on, say, AWS GPUs, or deploying your trained model to other systems (for example, a recommendation system integrated into a news website) is a critical step. You will improve your training time and extend the amount of computing that can be used. This means being able to experiment with more complex models too. Ideally, we would want a library that makes it easy to integrate with existing tools or has tools of its own.

Now that we've got a reasonable set of requirements for our ideal library, let's take a look at a number of the popular options out there in the community. The following list is by no means exhaustive; however, it covers most of the major ML-related Go projects on GitHub, from the most narrow to the most general.

ML libraries

We will now consider each of the main ML libraries, assessing their utility based on the criteria we defined earlier, including any negative aspects or shortcomings.

Word-embeddings in Go

Word-embeddings in Go is an example of a task-specific ML library. It implements the two-layer neural network necessary to generate word embeddings, using `Word2vec` and `GloVe`. It is a great implementation, fast, and clean. It implements a limited number of features very well and in ways specific to the task of generating word embeddings via `Word2vec` and `GloVe`.

An example of this is a core feature required for training DNNs, an optimization method called SGD. This is used in the `GloVe` model, developed by a team at Stanford. However, the code is integrated specifically with the `GloVe` model, and the additional optimization methods used in `Word2Vec` (negative sampling and skip-gram) are not useful with DNNs.

This can be useful for DL tasks, say, for generating an embedded layer or dense vector representation of a text corpus that can be used in **Long Short-Term Memory (LSTM)** networks, which we will cover in `Chapter 5`, *Next Word Prediction with Recurrent Neural Networks*. However, all of the advanced functions we would need (for example, gradient descent or backpropagation) and model features (LSTM units themselves) are absent.

Naive Bayesian classification and genetic algorithms for Go or Golang

These two libraries form another set of task-specific examples of ML libraries in Go. Both are well-written and offer primitives specific to their features, but these primitives do not generalize. In the Naive Bayes classifier `lib`, matrices are built manually before they can be used, while the traditional approach to generic algorithms makes no use of matrices at all. There has been some work on incorporating them into GA; however, this work is yet to make it into the GA library we're referencing here.

ML for Go

A library that has a more general collection of useful features is GoLearn. While DL-specific features are on its wish list, it has the necessary primitives to implement simple neural networks, random forests, clustering, and other ML approaches. It relies heavily on Gonum, a library that provides implementations of `float64` and `complex128` matrix structures and linear algebra operations on them.

Let's look at what this means from a code perspective, as shown here:

```
type Network struct {
        origWeights *mat.Dense
        weights *mat.Dense // n * n
        biases []float64 // n for each neuron
        funcs []NeuralFunction // for each neuron
        size int
        input int
    }
```

Here, we have GoLearn's primary definition of what a neural network looks like. It contains definitions for weights using Gonum's `mat` library to create the weights as dense matrices. It has biases, functions, size, and input, all of the essentials of a basic feedforward network. (We will cover feedforward networks in `Chapter 3`, *Beyond Basic Neural Networks – Autoencoders and RBMs*).

What is lacking is the ability to easily define connections within and across layers (for advanced network architectures, such as RNNs and their derivatives, and functions essential for DL, such as convolution operations and batch normalization). Coding these by hand would add a significant amount of development time to your project, which is to say nothing of the time needed to optimize their performance.

Another big missing feature, and for training and scaling the network architectures used in DL, is CUDA support. We will go through CUDA in Chapter 4, *CUDA – GPU-Accelerated Training*, but without this support, we will be limited to simple models that do not use massive quantities of data, that is, the kind we are interested in for the purposes of this book.

Machine learning libraries for Golang

This library differs in that it implements its own matrix operations and does not rely on Gonum. It is really a collection of implementations that include the following:

- Linear regression
- Logistic regression
- Neural networks
- Collaborative filtering
- Gaussian multivariate distribution for anomaly detection systems

Individually, these are powerful tools; indeed, linear regression is often described as one of the most important tools in the data scientist's toolkit, but, for our purposes, we really only care about the neural networks portion of the library. And here, we see limitations similar to those of GoLearn, such as limited activation functions and a lack of tools for intra- and interlayer connections (for example, LSTM units).

The author has an additional library that implements CUDA matrix operations; however, both this and the go_ml library itself have not been updated in four years (at the time of writing), so this is not a project you could simply import and start building neural networks straightaway.

GoBrain

Another library that is not under active development is GoBrain. You might then ask: why bother reviewing it? Briefly, it is of interest because it is the only other library apart from Gorgonia that attempts to implement primitives from more advanced network architectures. Specifically, it extends its primary network, which is a basic feedforward neural network, to become something new, an **Elman recurrent neural network**, or **SRN**.

Introduced in 1990, this was the first network architecture to include recurrence, or loops, connecting hidden layers of a network and adjacent *context* units. This had the effect of allowing networks to learn sequence dependencies, such as the *context* of a word, or potentially the grammar and syntax of human language. Groundbreaking for its time, the SRN offered *the vision that these units might be emergent consequences of a learning process operating over the latent structure in the speech stream.*

SRNs have given way to more modern recurrent neural networks, which we will cover in detail in Chapter 5, *Next Word Prediction with Recurrent Neural Networks*. However, in GoBrain, we have an interesting example of a library that contains the beginnings of what we need for our work.

A set of numeric libraries for the Go programming language

The most feature-complete library that could potentially be useful for DL (aside from Gorgonia, which we will cover in later sections) is Gonum. The simplest description would be that Gonum attempts to emulate much of the functionality of the well-known scientific computing libraries in Python, namely, NumPy and SciPy.

Let's take a look at a code example for constructing a matrix we might use to represent inputs to a DNN.

Initialize a matrix and back it with some numbers, as follows:

```
// Initialize a matrix of zeros with 3 rows and 4 columns.
d := mat.NewDense(3, 4, nil)
fmt.Printf("%v\n", mat.Formatted(d))
// Initialize a matrix with pre-allocated data. Data has row-major storage.
data := []float64{
    6, 3, 5,
    -1, 9, 7,
    2, 3, 4,}
d2 := mat.NewDense(3, 3, data)
fmt.Printf("%v\n", mat.Formatted(d2))
```

Perform operations on the matrix, as shown in the following code:

```
a := mat.NewDense(2, 3, []float64{
    3, 4, 5,
    1, 2, 3,
})

b := mat.NewDense(3, 3, []float64{    1, 1, 8,
```

```
    1, 2, -3,
    5, 5, 7,
})
fmt.Println("tr(b) =", mat.Trace(b))

c := mat.Dense{}
c.Mul(a, b)
c.Add(c, a)
c.Mul(c, b.T())
fmt.Printf("%v\n", mat.Formatted(c))
```

Here, we can see that Gonum offers us the primitives we need to manipulate the matrices exchanged between layers in DNNs, namely, `c.Mul` and `c.Add`.

When we decide to scale up our design ambitions, this is when we run into the limitations of Gonum. There are no GRU/LSTM cells and there is no SGD with backpropagation. If we are to reliably and efficiently construct DNNs that we want to carry all of the way through to production, we need to look elsewhere for a more complete library.

Using Gorgonia

At the time of writing this book, there are two libraries that would typically be considered for DL in Go, TensorFlow and Gorgonia. However, while TensorFlow is definitely well regarded and has a full-featured API in Python, this is not the case in Go. As discussed previously, the Go bindings for TensorFlow are only suited to loading models that have already been created in Python, but not for creating models from scratch.

Gorgonia has been built from the ground up to be a Go library that is able to both train ML models and perform inference. This is a particularly valuable property, especially if you have an existing Go application or you are looking to build a Go application. Gorgonia allows you to develop, train, and maintain your DL model in your existing Go environment. For this book, we will be using Gorgonia exclusively to build models.

Before we go on to build models, let's go through some basics of Gorgonia and learn how to build simple equations in it.

The basics of Gorgonia

Gorgonia is a lower-level library, which means that we need to build the equations and the architecture for models ourselves. This means that there isn't a built-in DNN classifier function that will magically create an entire model with several hidden layers and immediately be ready to apply to your dataset.

Gorgonia facilitates DL by being a library that makes working with multidimensional arrays easy. It does this by providing loads of operators to work with so you can build the underlying mathematical equations that make up layers in a DL model. We can then proceed to use these layers in our model.

Another important feature of Gorgonia is performance. By removing the need to think about how to optimize tensor operations, we can focus on building the model and ensuring the architecture is correct, rather than worrying about whether or not our model will be performant.

As Gorgonia is a little lower-level than a typical ML library, building a model takes a few more steps. However, this does not mean that building a model in Gorgonia is difficult. It requires the following three basic steps:

1. Create a computation graph
2. Input the data
3. Execute the graph

Wait, what's a computation graph? A **computation graph** is a directed graph where each of the nodes is either an operation or a variable. Variables can be fed into operations, which will then produce a value. This value can then be fed into another operation. In more familiar terms, a graph is like a function that takes all of the variables and then produces a result.

A variable can be anything; we can make it a single scalar value, a vector (that is, an array), or a matrix. In DL, we typically work with a more generalized structure called a tensor; a tensor can be thought of as something similar to an n-dimensional matrix.

The following screenshot shows a visual representation of *n*-dimensional tensors:

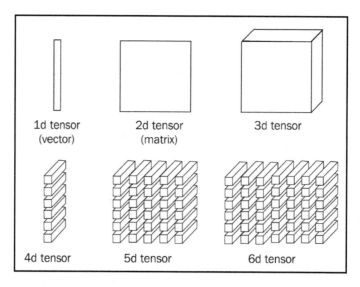

We represent equations as graphs because this makes it easier for us to optimize the performance of our model. This is enabled by the fact that, by putting each node in a directed graph, we have a good idea of what its dependencies are. Since we model each node as an independent piece of code, we know that all it needs to execute are its dependencies (which can be other nodes or other variables). Also, as we traverse the graph, we can know which nodes are independent of each other and run those concurrently.

For example, take the following diagram:

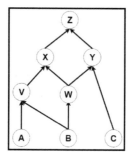

As **A**, **B**, and **C** are independent, we can easily compute these concurrently. The computation of **V** requires both **A** and **B** to be ready. However, **W** only requires **B** to be ready. This follows into the next level, and so on, up until we are ready to compute the final output in **Z**.

Simple example – addition

The easiest way to understand how this all fits together is by building a simple example.

To start, let's implement a simple graph to add two numbers together—basically, this would be: $c = a + b$:

1. First, let's import some libraries—most importantly, Gorgonia, as follows:

```
package main
import (
        "fmt"
        "log"
        . "gorgonia.org/gorgonia"
    )
```

2. Then, let's start our main function, like so:

```
func main() {
   g := NewGraph()
}
```

3. To that, let's add our scalars, as shown here:

```
a = NewScalar(g, Float64, WithName("a"))
b = NewScalar(g, Float64, WithName("b"))
```

4. Then, very importantly, let's define our operation node, as follows:

```
c, err = Add(a, b)
if err != nil {
                log.Fatal(err)
                }
```

Note that c will not actually have a value now; we've just defined a new node of our computation graph, so we need to execute it before it will have a value.

5. To execute it, we need to create a virtual machine object for it to run in, as follows:

```
machine := NewTapeMachine(g)
```

6. Then, set the initial values of a and b, and proceed to get the machine to execute our graph, as shown here:

```
Let(a, 1.0)
Let(b, 2.0)
```

```
                    if machine.RunAll() != nil {
                                        log.Fatal(err)
                                        }
```

The complete code is as follows:

```
package main

import (
        "fmt"
        "log"

        . "gorgonia.org/gorgonia"
)

func main() {
        g := NewGraph()

        var a, b, c *Node
        var err error

        // define the expression
        a = NewScalar(g, Float64, WithName("a"))
        b = NewScalar(g, Float64, WithName("b"))
        c, err = Add(a, b)
        if err != nil {
                log.Fatal(err)
        }

        // create a VM to run the program on
        machine := NewTapeMachine(g)

        // set initial values then run
        Let(a, 1.0)
        Let(b, 2.0)
        if machine.RunAll() != nil {
                log.Fatal(err)
        }

        fmt.Printf("%v", c.Value())
        // Output: 3.0
}
```

Now, we have built our first computation graph in Gorgonia and executed it!

Vectors and matrices

Of course, being able to add to numbers isn't why we're here; we're here to work with tensors, and eventually, DL equations, so let's take the first step toward something a little more complicated.

The goal here is to now create a graph that will compute the following simple equation:

$$z = Wx$$

Note that W is an $n \times n$ matrix, and x is a vector of size n. For the purposes of this example, we will use $n = 2.1957$.

Again, we start with the same basic main function, as shown here:

```
package main

import (
        "fmt"
        "log"

        G "gorgonia.org/gorgonia"
        "gorgonia.org/tensor"
)

func main() {
        g := NewGraph()
}
```

You'll notice that we've chosen to alias the Gorgonia package as G.

We then create our first tensor, the matrix, W, like so:

```
matB := []float64{0.9,0.7,0.4,0.2}
matT := tensor.New(tensor.WithBacking(matB), tensor.WithShape(2, 2))
mat := G.NewMatrix(g,
        tensor.Float64,
        G.WithName("W"),
        G.WithShape(2, 2),
        G.WithValue(matT),
)
```

You'll notice that we've done things a bit differently this time around, as listed here:

1. We've started by declaring an array with the values that we want in our matrix
2. We've then created a tensor from that matrix with a shape of 2 x 2, as we want a 2 x 2 matrix
3. After all of that, we've then created a new node in our graph for the matrix, given it the name W, and initialized it with the value of the tensor

We then create our second tensor and input node the same way, the vector, x, as follows:

```
vecB := []float64{5,7}

vecT := tensor.New(tensor.WithBacking(vecB), tensor.WithShape(2))

vec := G.NewVector(g,
        tensor.Float64,
        G.WithName("x"),
        G.WithShape(2),
        G.WithValue(vecT),
)
```

Just like last time, we then add an operator node, z, that will multiply the two (instead of an addition operation):

```
z, err := G.Mul(mat, vec)
```

Then, as last time, create a new tape machine and run it, as shown here, and then print the result:

```
machine := G.NewTapeMachine(g)
if machine.RunAll() != nil {
        log.Fatal(err)
}
fmt.Println(z.Value().Data())
// Output: [9.4 3.4]
```

Visualizing the graph

In many cases, it is also very useful to visualize the graph; you can easily do this by adding io or ioutil to your imports and the following line to your code:

```
ioutil.WriteFile("simple_graph.dot", []byte(g.ToDot()), 0644)
```

This will produce a DOT file; you can open this in GraphViz, or, more conveniently, convert it to an SVG. You can view it in most modern browsers by installing GraphViz and entering the following in the command line:

```
dot -Tsvg simple_graph.dot -O
```

This will produce simple_graph.dot.svg; you can open this in your browser to see a rendering of the graph, as follows:

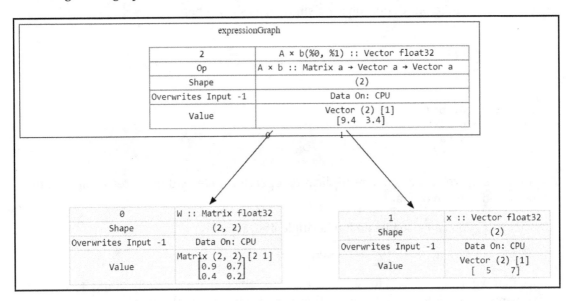

You can see, in our graph, that we have two inputs, W and x, and this then gets fed into our operator, being a matrix multiplication with a vector giving us the result as well—another vector.

Building more complex expressions

Of course, we've mostly covered how to build simple equations; however, what happens if your equation is a little bit more complicated, for example, like the following:

$$z = Wx + b$$

We can also very easily do this by changing our code a bit to add the following line:

```
b := G.NewScalar(g,
        tensor.Float64,
        G.WithName("b"),
        G.WithValue(3.0)
)
```

Then, we can change our definition for z slightly, as shown here:

```
a, err := G.Mul(mat, vec)
if err != nil {
        log.Fatal(err)
}

z, err := G.Add(a, b)
if err != nil {
        log.Fatal(err)
}
```

As you can see, we've created a multiplication operator node, and then created an addition operator node on top of that.

Alternatively, you can also just do it in a single line, as follows:

```
z, err := G.Add(G.Must(G.Mul(mat, vec)), b)
```

Notice that we use Must here to suppress the error object; we are merely doing it here for convenience, as we know that the operation to add this node to the graph will work. It is important to note that you may want to restructure this code to create the node for addition separately so that you can have error handling for each step.

If you now proceed to build and execute the code, you will find that it will produce the following:

```
// Output: [12.4 6.4]
```

The computation graph now looks like the following screenshot:

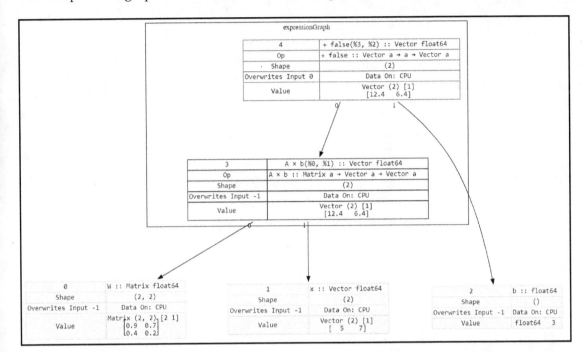

You can see that W and x both feed into the first operation (our multiplication operation) and then, later, it feeds into our addition operation to produce our results.

That's an introduction to using Gorgonia! As you can now hopefully see, it is a library that contains the necessary primitives that will allow us to build the first simple, and then more complicated, neural networks in the following chapters.

Summary

This chapter included a brief introduction to DL, both its history and applications. It was followed by a discussion of why Go is a great language for DL and demonstrated how the library we use in Gorgonia compares to other libraries in Go.

The next chapter will cover the magic that makes neural networks and DL work, which includes activation functions, network structure, and training algorithms.

2
What Is a Neural Network and How Do I Train One?

While we've now discussed Go and the libraries available for it, we haven't yet discussed what constitutes a neural network. Toward the end of the previous chapter, we used Gorgonia to construct a graph that, when executed by an appropriate VM, performs several basic operations (specifically, addition and multiplication) on a series of matrices and vectors.

We will now talk about how to build a neural network and get it working. This will teach you about the components necessary to build the more advanced neural network architectures we will be discussing later in this book.

This chapter will cover the following topics:

- A basic neural network
- Activation functions
- Gradient descent and backpropagation
- Advanced gradient descent algorithms

A basic neural network

Let's first build a simple neural network. This network will use the basic operations of addition and multiplication to take a 4 x 3 matrix of integers, initialize a weight coefficient represented by a 3 x 1 column vector, and gradually adjust those weights until they predict, for a given sequence of inputs (and after the application of a Sigmoid nonlinearity), an output that matches the validation dataset.

The structure of a neural network

The purpose of this example is clearly not to build a cutting-edge computer vision system but, rather, to demonstrate how to use these fundamental operations (and how Gorgonia handles them) in the context of a parameterized function where the parameters are learned over time. The key goal of this section is to understand the idea of a network that learns. This *learning* really just means the continuous, deliberate re-parameterization of the network (updating the weights). This is done by an optimization method that is, essentially, a small amount of code representing some basic undergraduate-level calculus.

The Sigmoid function (and activation functions more generally), **Stochastic Gradient Descent (SGD)**, and backpropagation will each receive detailed treatment in later sections of this chapter. For now, we will talk about them in the context of the code; that is, where and how they are used and what their role is in the function we are computing.

By the time you reach the end of this book, or if you are an experienced ML practitioner, the following will look like an absurdly simple first step into the world of neural network architectures. But if this is your first rodeo, pay close attention. All of the fundamentals that make the magic happen are here.

What is the network made of? The following are the major components of our toy example neural network:

- **Input data**: This is a 4 x 3 matrix.
- **Validation data**: This is a 1 x 4 column vector, or in reality, a four-rowed matrix with one column. This is expressed in Gorgonia as `WithShape(4,1)`.
- **An activation (Sigmoid) function**: This introduces nonlinearity into our network and the function we are learning.
- **A synapse**: This is also called a **trainable weight**, which is the key parameter of the network we will be optimizing with SGD.

Each of these components and their associated operations are represented as nodes on our computational graph. As we move through the explanation of what the network is doing, we will generate visualizations of the graph using the techniques we learned in Chapter 1, *Introduction to Deep Learning in Go*.

We are also going to over-engineer our network a little. What does this mean? Consider the following chunk of code:

```
type nn struct {
    g *ExprGraph
    w0, w1 *Node
```

```
    pred *Node
}
```

We are embedding the key components of the network in a `struct` named nn. This not only makes our code readable, but it scales well when we want to perform our optimization process (SGD/backpropagation) on a number of weights for each layer of a deep (many-layered) network. As you can see, beyond the weights for each layer, we also have a node representing the prediction our network makes, as well as `*ExprGraph` itself.

Our network has two layers. These are computed during the forward pass of our network. A forward pass represents all of the numerical transformations we want to perform on the value nodes in our computation graph.

Specifically, we have the following:

- `10`: The input matrix, our X
- `w0`: The trainable parameter, our network weight that will be optimized by the SGD algorithm
- `11`: The value of the Sigmoid applied to the dot product of `10` and `w0`
- `pred`: A node that represents the *prediction* of the network, fed back to the appropriate field in `nn struct`

So, what are we aiming to achieve here?

We want to build a system that learns a function that best models the columnar sequence of 0, 0, 1, 1. Time to dive in!

Your first neural network

Let's start with the basic naming our package and importing the packages we will need. This process is carried out in the following steps:

1. For this example, we will be using a `tensor` library provided by the same developers as Gorgonia. We will use it for the backing tensors that are attached to their respective nodes in the computation graph:

```
package main

import (
    "fmt"
    "io/ioutil"
    "log"
```

```
.   "gorgonia.org/gorgonia"
    "gorgonia.org/tensor"
)
```

2. Create a variable that will catch errors with the following code:

```
var err error
```

We can now define the main `struct` for embedding the neural network's graph, weights, and prediction (output). In a deeper network, we would have `w0`, `w1`, `w2`, `w3`, and so on, until `wn`. There are additional network parameters we might capture in this `struct`, which we will cover in detail in later chapters. For example, in a **Convolutional Neural Network (CNN)**, you would also have the per-layer dropout probabilities, which assist us in preventing our network from *overfitting* to our training data. The point here is that no matter how advanced the architecture or how new the paper, you could conceivably scale up the following `struct` to express the properties of any network:

```
type nn struct {
    g *ExprGraph
    w0, w1 *Node

    pred *Node
}
```

Now, we'll consider the method to instantiate a new nn. Here, we create the node for our weight matrix or, in this specific case, our row vector. This process generalizes to the creation of any node we are backing with an *n*-rank tensor.

The following method returns `ExprGraph` with the new node attached:

```
func newNN(g *ExprGraph) *nn {
    // Create node for w/weight (needs fixed values replaced with random
values w/mean 0)
    wB := []float64{-0.167855599, 0.44064899, -0.99977125}
    wT := tensor.New(tensor.WithBacking(wB), tensor.WithShape(3, 1))
    w0 := NewMatrix(g,
        tensor.Float64,
        WithName("w"),
        WithShape(3, 1),
        WithValue(wT),
    )
    return nn{
        g: g,
        w0: w0,
    }
}
```

Now that we have added a node to the graph and backed it with a real-valued tensor, we should inspect our computational graph to see how this weight appears, as shown in the following table:

0	w :: Matrix float64
Shape	(3, 1)
Overwrites Input -1	Data On: CPU
Value	Vector (3, 1) [1 1] C[-0.168 0.441 -1]

The properties to notice here are the type (a matrix of `float64`), `Shape` of (3, 1), and, of course, the three values occupying this vector. This is not much of a graph; indeed, our node is lonely, but we will add to it soon. In more complex networks, there will be a node backed by a weight matrix for each layer we use.

Before we do this, we must add another feature that will allow us to scale our code to these more complex networks. Here, we are defining the network's learnables, key for computing the gradient. It is this list of nodes that the `Grad()` function will operate on. Grouping these nodes in such a way allows us to calculate the gradients for the weights across *n*-layers of our network in a single function. Scaling this just means adding `w1`, `w2`, `w3`, and `wn`, as shown in the following code:

```
func (m *nn) learnables() Nodes {
    return Nodes{m.w0}
}
```

Now, we are getting to the core part of the network. The following function, *when executed*, will expand our graph with operations and nodes representing the input and hidden layer. It is important to note that, of course, this is a function that will be called in the main part of our network; for now, we are defining it upfront:

```
func (m *nn) fwd(x *Node) (err error) {
    var l0, l1 *Node

    // Set first layer to be copy of input
    l0 = x

    // Dot product of l0 and w0, use as input for Sigmoid
    l0dot := Must(Mul(l0, m.w0))

    // Build hidden layer out of result
    l1 = Must(Sigmoid(l0dot))
    // fmt.Println("l1: \n", l1.Value())
```

```
        m.pred = 11
        return

    }
```

We can see the application of the `Sigmoid` function on the hidden layer, `11`, as we briefly discussed when elaborating the components of our network. We will cover it in detail in the next section of this chapter.

We can now write our `main` function where we will instantiate our network and all of the various methods described previously. Let's step through it in detail. The first step of this process is shown in the following code:

```
func main() {
    rand.Seed(31337)

    intercept Ctrl+C
    sigChan := make(chan os.Signal, 1)
    signal.Notify(sigChan, syscall.SIGINT, syscall.SIGTERM)
    doneChan := make(chan bool, 1)

    // Create graph and network
    g := NewGraph()
    m := newNN(g)
```

Next, we define our input matrix, as follows:

```
    // Set input x to network
    xB := []float64{0, 0, 1, 0, 1, 1, 1, 0, 1, 1, 1, 1}
    xT := tensor.New(tensor.WithBacking(xB), tensor.WithShape(4, 3))
    x := NewMatrix(g,
        tensor.Float64,
        WithName("X"),
        WithShape(4, 3),
        WithValue(xT),
    )
```

Then, we define what will effectively be our validation dataset, like so:

```
    // Define validation dataset
    yB := []float64{0, 0, 1, 1}
    yT := tensor.New(tensor.WithBacking(yB), tensor.WithShape(4, 1))
    y := NewMatrix(g,
        tensor.Float64,
        WithName("y"),
        WithShape(4, 1),
        WithValue(yT),
    )
```

Let's take a look at what our graph looks like now with the addition of X and y:

			1	X :: Matrix float64			2	y :: Matrix float64
0	w :: Matrix float64		Shape	(4, 3)			Shape	(4, 1)
Shape	(3, 1)		Overwrites Input -1	Data On: CPU			Overwrites Input -1	Data On: CPU
Overwrites Input -1	Data On: CPU			Matrix (4, 3) [3 1]			Value	Vector (4, 1) [1 1] C[0 0 1 1]
Value	Vector (3, 1) [1 1] C[-0.168 0.441 -1]		Value	⌈ 0 0 1 ⌉ | 0 1 1 | | 1 0 1 | ⌊ 1 1 1 ⌋				

We can see the individual nodes, w, X, and y. As we did when we looked at w, note the type, Shape, and Value of each.

Now, we call the fwd method of our nn and really build out our graph to include the computational relationships between X, y and w, as shown in the following code:

```
// Run forward pass
if err = m.fwd(x); err != nil {
    log.Fatalf("%+v", err)
}
```

This is where the process of optimization begins. Our network has made its first prediction, so we will now define and compute a cost function that will allow us to determine how wrong our weights are and, later, how much we need to adjust the weights by to get us closer to the target, y (our validation dataset). In this example, we will repeat this process a fixed number of times to allow this relatively simple network to converge.

The following code first computes the loss (that is, *how much did we miss by?*). Then, we take cost as Mean of the validation data:

```
losses := Must(Sub(y, m.pred))
cost := Must(Mean(losses))
```

Let's also create var to track the change in cost over time, like so:

```
var costVal Value
Read(cost, costVal)
```

Before we go ahead and calculate the gradients in our network, let's produce a visualization of the state of our graph using the following line of code, which should, by now, look familiar:

```
ioutil.WriteFile("pregrad.dot", []byte(g.ToDot()), 0644)
```

Convert into PNG using the following line:

```
dot -Tpng pregrad.dot  -O
```

We now have a graph that connects the nodes that contain our data (input, weights, and validation) and the operations we will be performing on them.

The graph is getting too large to include in a single page, so we will now consider only the important parts of this step. Firstly, note that our weight node now has a `Grad` field that currently has no value (a forward pass has been run, but we are yet to calculate the gradients), as shown in the following table:

0	w :: Matrix float64
Shape	(3, 1)
Overwrites Input -1	Data On: CPU
Value	Grad
Vector (3, 1) [1 1] C[-0.168 0.441 -1]	%!s(NIL)
Ptr: 0x842351307104x	Ptr:

We also now have a number of gradient operations; here's an excerpt in the following diagram:

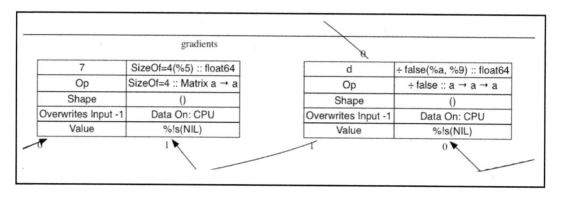

Now, let's compute the gradient, the cost relative to the weights (represented as `m.learnables`). This step is shown in the following code:

```
if _, err = Grad(cost, m.learnables()...); err != nil {
    log.Fatal(err)
}
```

We can now instantiate the VM that will be processing our graph. We also select our `solver`, in this case, a vanilla SGD, as shown in the following:

```
// Instantiate VM and Solver
vm := NewTapeMachine(g, BindDualValues(m.learnables()...))
solver := NewVanillaSolver(WithLearnRate(0.001), WithClip(5))
// solver := NewRMSPropSolver()
```

A new option we're providing our `vm` with is `BindDualValues`. This option ensures that the gradients we calculate are bound to the node that contains the value for which the derivative is being obtained. This means that, instead of the node saying, *go to node x to find the value of the gradient*, the value is immediately accessible to `vm`. This is what the change to our weight node looks like on the graph:

0	w :: Matrix float64
Shape	(3, 1)
Overwrites Input -1	Data On: CPU
Value	Grad
Vector (3, 1) [1 1] C[-0.168 0.441 -0.999]	Vector (3, 1) [1 1] C[0 0 0]
Ptr: 0x842350578400x	Ptr: 0xc42025b0c0

The `Value` field now contains the partial derivative of the output with respect to the node. We are now finally ready to run our full training loop. For a simple example such as this, we will run the loop an arbitrary number of times, specifically, `10000` loops, as shown in the following example:

```
for i := 0; i < 10000; i++ {
    if err = vm.RunAll(); err != nil {
        log.Fatalf("Failed at inter %d: %v", i, err)
    }
    solver.Step(NodesToValueGrads(m.learnables()))
    fmt.Println("\nState at iter", i)
    fmt.Println("Cost: \n", cost.Value())
    fmt.Println("Weights: \n", m.w0.Value())
    // vm.Set(m.w0, wUpd)
    // vm.Reset()
}
fmt.Println("Output after Training: \n", m.pred.Value())
}
```

While we are already familiar with the idea of using a VM to compute our graph, we have added a step here of calling `solver`, which we defined previously. `Step` works its way through the sequence of trainable nodes (that is, our weights), adding the gradient and multiplying it by the learn rate we specified previously.

And that's it! Now, we run our program and expect a post-training output of 0, 0, 1, 1, as shown in the following code:

```
Output after Training:
C [[0.00966449][0.00786506][0.99358898][0.99211957]]
```

That's close enough to declare that our network has converged!

Activation functions

Now that you know how to build a basic neural network, let's go through the purpose of some of the elements of your model. One of those elements was the *Sigmoid*, which is an activation function. Sometimes these are also called **transfer functions**.

As you have learned previously, a given layer can be simply defined as weights applied to inputs; add some bias and then decide on activation. An activation function decides whether a neuron is *fired*. We also put this into the network to help to create more complex relationships between input and output. While doing this, we also need it to be a function that works with our backpropagation, so that we can easily optimize our weighs via an optimization method (that is, gradient descent). This means that we need the output of the function to be differentiable.

There are a few things to consider when choosing an activation function, as follows:

- **Speed**: Simple activation functions are quicker to execute than more complex activation functions. This is important since, in deep learning, we tend to run the model through large amounts of data, and therefore, will be executing each function over a reasonably large dataset many times.
- **Differentiability**: As we have already noted, being able to differentiate the function is useful during backpropagation. Having a gradient allows us to adjust our weights in a direction that brings our network closer to convergence. In brief, it allows us to calculate errors to improve our model by minimizing our cost function.

- **Continuity**: It should return a value across the entire range of the inputs.
- **Monotonicity**: While this property is not strictly necessary, it helps to optimize the neural network since it will converge faster during gradient descent. Using non-monotonic functions is possible, but we are likely to run into longer training times overall.

Step functions

Of course, the most basic activation function would be a step function. If the value of x is more than a fixed value, a, then y is either 0 or 1, as shown in the following code:

```
func step(x) {
    if x >= 0 {
        return 1
    } else {
        return 0
    }
}
```

As you can see in the following diagram, the step function is extremely simple; it takes a value and then returns 0 or 1:

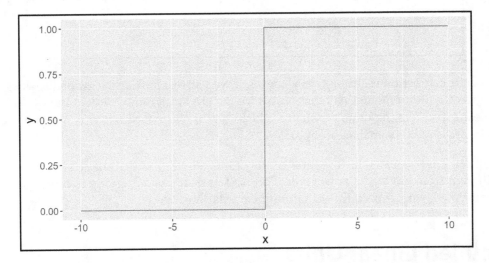

This is a very simple function and one that is not particularly useful for deep learning. This is because the gradient of this function is a constant zero, meaning that, when we are doing backpropagation, it will constantly produce zeroes, which results in very little (if any at all) improvement when we are performing backpropagation.

Linear functions

A possible extension to the `step` function might be to use a `linear` function, as shown in the following code:

```
func linear(x){
    return 0.5 * x
}
```

This is still very simple and, if we were to chart it out, it would look something like the following diagram:

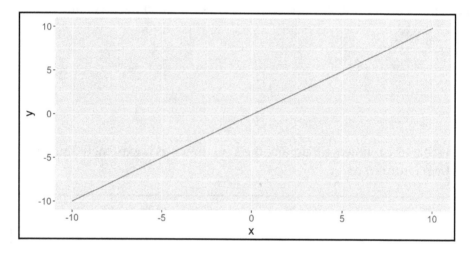

However, this function is still not very useful. If we were to look at the gradient, we'll see that, when we differentiate this function, all we get is a straight line equal to the value of `a`. This means it suffers the same problem as the `step` function; that is to say, we won't see much improvement from backpropagation.

In addition, if we were to stack several layers of this, you'll find that really all we get is not too different from having just one layer. This isn't useful if we are trying to build models with multiple layers, especially with non-linear relationships.

Rectified Linear Units

Rectified Linear Unit (ReLU) is the most popular activation function in use. We will be using it as the primary activation function in a number of advanced architectures in later chapters.

It can be described as follows:

```
func relu(x){
    return Max(0,x)
}
```

If we were to chart it out, it looks something like the following diagram:

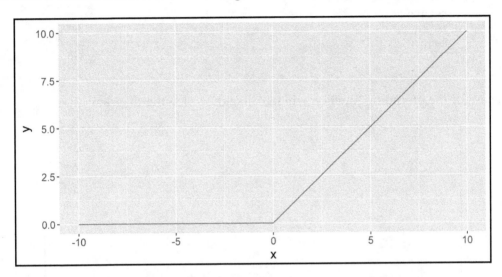

As you can see, it is extremely similar to a linear function, except that it goes to zero (therefore indicating that the neuron is not activated).

ReLU also has many useful properties, as follows:

- **It is nonlinear**: Therefore, stacking several layers of these will not necessarily result in being the same as one layer
- **It is differentiable**: Therefore, it works with backpropagation
- **It is quick**: It calculates quickly, which is important when we are running this calculation numerous times across layers or training passes of our network

ReLU goes to zero if the input is negative. This can be useful, since this results in fewer neurons being activated, and, therefore, this can potentially speed up our calculations. However, since it can result in 0, this can very quickly cause a neuron to *die* and never activate again, given certain inputs.

Leaky ReLU

We can modify the ReLU function to have a small gradient when the input is negative—this can very quickly be accomplished, as follows:

```
func leaky_relu(x) {
    if x >= 0 {
        return x
    } else {
        return 0.01 * x
    }
}
```

The chart for the preceding function will look like the following diagram:

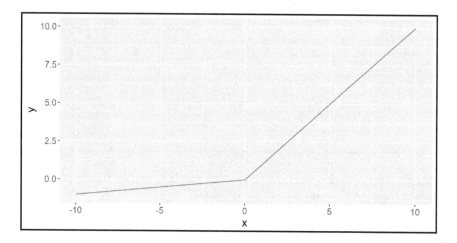

Note that this chart has been altered for emphasis, so the slope of y with respect to x is actually 0.1 instead of 0.01, as is typical for what is considered a leaky ReLU.

As it will always produce a small gradient, this should help to prevent the neuron from *dying* on a more permanent basis while still giving us many of the benefits of ReLU.

Sigmoid functions

A Sigmoid or logistic function is also relatively popular, as shown here:

```
func sigmoid(x){
    return 1 / (1 + Exp(-x))
}
```

The output is as follows:

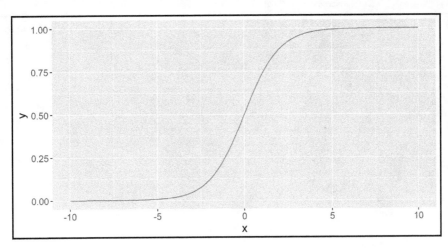

Sigmoid has a property that is also useful: it can map any real number back down to a range between 0 and 1. This can be very useful for producing models that prefer an output between 0 and 1 (for example, a model for predicting the probability of something).

It also has most of the properties we are looking for, as listed here:

- It is **nonlinear**. Therefore, stacking several layers of these will not necessarily result in being the same as one layer.
- It is **differentiable**. Therefore, it works with backpropagation.
- It is **monotonic**.

However, one drawback is that it is more costly to compute compared to ReLU, and therefore, it will take longer overall to train a model with this.

Tanh

It can also be helpful to have a steeper gradient during training; as such, we can use the tanh function instead of the Sigmoid function, as shown in the following code:

```
func tanh(x){
    return 2 * (1 + Exp(-2*x)) - 1
}
```

We get the following output:

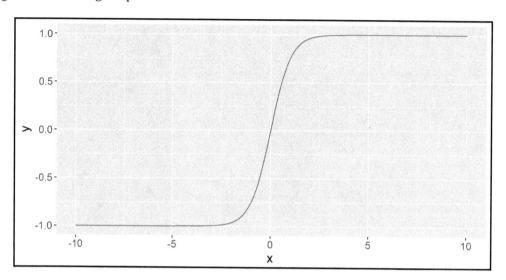

The `tanh` function has another useful property: its slope is much steeper than the `Sigmoid` function; this helps networks with `tanh` activation functions to descend the gradient faster when adjusting weights. The output for both functions is plotted in the following output:

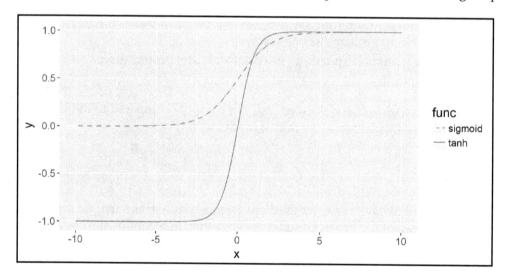

But which one should we use?

Each of these activation functions is useful; however, as ReLU has the most useful features of all of the activation functions and is easy to calculate, this should be the function you are using most of the time.

It can be a good idea to switch to leaky ReLU if you run into stuck gradients frequently. However, you can usually lower the learning rate to help to prevent this or use it in the earlier layers, instead of all of your layers, in order to maintain the edge of having fewer activations overall across the network.

`Sigmoid` is most valuable as an output layer, preferably with a probability as the output. The `tanh` function can also be valuable, for example, where we would like layers to constantly adjust values upward and downward (rather than being biased upward like ReLU and Sigmoid).

So, the short answer is: it depends on your network and the kind of output you are expecting.

It should, however, be noted that while a number of activation functions have been presented here for you to consider, other activation functions have been proposed such as PReLU, softmax, and Swish, which can also be considered, depending on the task at hand. This is still an active area of research and is considered to be far from solved, so stay tuned!

Gradient descent and backpropagation

We've talked about backpropagation and gradient descent in the context of example code in the first section of this chapter, but it can be hard to really understand the concepts at play when Gorgonia is doing a lot of the heavy lifting for us. So, we will now take a look at the actual process itself.

Gradient descent

Backpropagation is how we really train our model; it's an algorithm we use to minimize the prediction error by adjusting our model's weights. We usually do this via a method called **gradient descent**.

Let's begin with a basic example—let's say we want to train a simple neural network to do the following, by multiplying a number by 0.5:

Input	Target
1	0.5
2	1.0
3	1.5
4	2.0

We have a basic model to start with, as follows:

$$y = W * x$$

So, to start, let's guess that W is actually two. The following table shows these results:

Input	Target	W * x
1	0.5	2
2	1.0	4
3	1.5	6
4	2.0	8

Now that we have the output of our *guess*, we can compare this *guess* to the answer we are expecting and calculate the relative error. For example, in this table, we are using the sum of the squared errors:

Input	Target	W * x	Absolute error	Squared error
1	0.5	2	-1.5	2.25
2	1.0	4	-3.0	9
3	1.5	6	-4.5	20.25
4	2.0	8	-6.0	36

By adding up the values in the last column of the preceding tables, we now have a sum of the squared errors, a total of 67.5.

We can certainly brute force all of the values from -10 to +10 to get an answer, but surely there must be a better way? Ideally, we want a more efficient way that scales to datasets that are not simple tables with four inputs.

A better method is to check the derivative (or gradient). One way we can do this is to do this same calculation again, but with a slightly higher weight; for example, let's try $W = 2.01$. The following table shows these results:

Input	Target	W * x	Absolute error	Squared error
1	0.5	2.01	-1.51	2.2801
2	1.0	4.02	-3.02	9.1204
3	1.5	6.03	-4.53	20.5209
4	2.0	8.04	-6.04	36.4816

This gives us a sum of the squared errors of 68.403; this is higher! This means that, intuitively, if we increase the weight, we're likely to see an increase in the error. The inverse is also true; if we decrease the weight, we are likely to see a decrease in the error. For example, let's try $W = 1.99$, as shown in the following table:

Input	Target	W * x	Absolute error	Squared error
0	0	0	0	0
4	2	4.04	-1.996	3.984016
8	4	8.08	-3.992	15.93606
16	8	15.84	-7.984	63.74426

This gives us a lower error of 83.66434.

If we were to plot the error for a given range of W, you can see that there is a natural bottom point. This is how we can descend on the gradient to minimize the errors.

For this specific example, we can easily plot the error as a function of our weights.

The goal is to follow the slope to the bottom, where the error is zero:

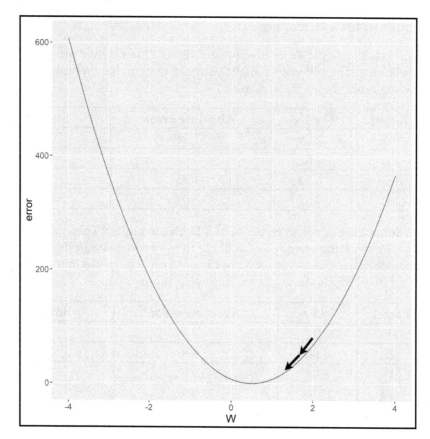

Let's try applying a weight update to our example to illustrate how this works. In general, we follow something called the **delta learning rule**, which is basically similar to the following:

$$new\_W = old\_W - eta * derivative$$

In this formula, *eta* is a constant, sometimes also called the **learning rate**. Recall that when we call `solver` in Gorgonia, we include a learning rate as one of the options, as shown here:

```
solver := NewVanillaSolver(WithLearnRate(0.001), WithClip(5))
```

You will also often see a 0.5 term added to the derivative for the error with respect to the output. This is because, if our error function is a square function, the derivative will be 2, so the 0.5 term is put there to cancel it out; however, *eta* is a constant anyway (so you can also just consider it absorbed into the *eta* term).

So, first, we need to work out what the derivative is for the error with respect to the output.

If we were to say that our learning rate was `0.001`, this makes our new weight the following:

```
new_W = 1.00 - 0.001 * 101.338
```

If we were to compute this, `new_W` would be `1.89866`. This is closer to our eventual target weight of 0.5, and, with enough repetition, we would eventually get there. You'll notice that our learning rate is small. If we set it too large (let's say, 1), we would've ended up adjusting our weight way too far into the negative instead, so we would end up going round and round our gradient, instead of descending it. Our choice of learning rate is important: too small and our model will take too long to converge, and too large and it may even diverge instead.

Backpropagation

This is a simple example. For complicated models with thousands, or even millions, of parameters across a number of layers, there are convolutional networks and we need to be more intelligent about how we propagate these updates back through our network. This is true for networks with a number of layers (increasing the number of parameters accordingly), with new research coming out that, in an extreme example, includes CNNs of 10,000 layers.

So, how can we go about this? The easiest way is to build your neural network out of functions for which we know the derivative. We can do this symbolically or on a more practical basis; if we build it out of functions where we know how to apply the function and where we know how to backpropagate (by virtue of knowing how to write a function for the derivative), we can build a neural network out of these functions.

Of course, building these functions can be time-consuming. Fortunately, Gorgonia already has all of these, hence allowing us to do what we call auto-differentiation. As I have mentioned previously, we create a directed graph for computation; this allows to do not only the forward pass but the backward pass as well!

For example, let's consider something with more layers (although still simple) like the following, where **i** is the input, **f** is the first layer with weight *w1*, **g** is the second layer with the weight, *w2*, and **o** is the output:

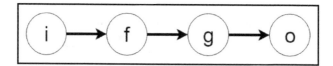

First, we have the error, which is a function of *o*. Let's call this *E*.

In order to update our weights in *g*, we need to know the derivative of the error with respect to the input of *g*.

From the chain rule when dealing with derivatives, we know that this is actually equivalent to the following:

$$dE\_dg = dE\_do * do\_dg * dg\_dw2$$

That is to say, the derivative of the error with respect to the input of *g* (*dE_dg*) is actually equivalent to the derivative of the error with respect to the output, (*dE_do*), multiplied by the derivative of the output with respect to the function, *g* (*do_dg*), and then multiplied by the derivative of the function, *g*, with respect to *w2*.

This gives us the derivative rate we need to update our weights in *g*.

We now need to do the same for *f*. How? It is a matter of repeating the process. We need the derivative of the error with respect to the input of *f*. Using the chain rule again, we know that the following is true:

$$dE\_df = dE\_do * do\_dg * dg\_df * df\_dw1$$

You'll notice that there is something in common here with the previous derivative, *dE_do* * *do_dg*.

This presents us with an opportunity for further optimization. We don't have to calculate the entirety of the derivative each time; we only need to know the derivative of the layer we are backpropagating from and the derivative of the layer we are backpropagating to, and this is true all of the way through the entire network. This is called the backpropagation algorithm, which allows us to update weights throughout our entire network without constantly needing to recalculate the derivatives of the error with respect to the specific weight that we are targeting from scratch, and we can reuse the result of previous calculations.

Stochastic gradient descent

We can further optimize the training process with a simple change. With basic (or batch) gradient descent, we calculate the adjustment by looking at the entire dataset. Therefore, the next obvious step for optimization is: can we calculate the adjustment by looking at less than the entire dataset?

As it turns out, the answer is yes! As we are expecting to train the network over numerous iterations, we can take advantage of the fact that we expect the gradient to be updated multiple times by calculating it for fewer examples. We can even do it by calculating it for a single example. By performing fewer calculations for each network update, we can significantly reduce the amount of computation required, meaning faster training times. This is essentially a stochastic approximation to gradient descent and, hence, how it got its name.

Advanced gradient descent algorithms

Now that we have an understanding of SGD and backpropagation, let's look at a number of advanced optimization methods (building on SGD) that offer us some kind of advantage, usually an improvement in training time (or the time it takes to minimize the cost function to the point where our network converges).

These *improved* methods include a general notion of velocity as an optimization parameter. Quoting from Wibisono and Wilson, in the opening to their paper on *Accelerated Methods in Optimization*:

> "In convex optimization, there is an acceleration phenomenon in which we can boost the convergence rate of certain gradient-based algorithms."

In brief, a number of these advanced algorithms all rely on a similar principle—that they can pass through local optima quickly, carried by their *momentum*—essentially, a moving average of our gradients.

Momentum

When thinking about optimization of gradient descent, we can certainly use intuition from real life to help to inform our methods. One example of this is momentum. If we imagine that most error gradients are really like a bowl, with the desired point in the middle, if we start from the highest point of the bowl, it could take us a long time to get to the bottom of the bowl.

If we think about some real-life physics, the steeper the side of the bowl, the quicker a ball would fall along the side as it gained momentum. Taking this as inspiration, we get what we can consider the momentum variation of SGD; we try to help to accelerate the descent down the gradient by considering that, if the gradient continues to go down the same direction, we give it more momentum. Alternatively, if we found that the gradient was changing direction, we'd reduce the amount of momentum.

While we don't want to get bogged down in heavy maths, there is a simple formula to calculate *momentum*. It is as follows:

$$V = momentum * m - lr * g$$

Here, m is the previous weight update, g is the current gradient with respect to parameter p, lr is the learning rate of our solver, and *momentum* is a constant.

So, if we want to understand exactly how to update our network parameters, we can adjust the formula in the following way:

$$P(new) = p + v = p + momentum * m - lr * g$$

What does this mean in practice? Let's look at some code.

Firstly, in Gorgonia, the basic interface for all optimization methods or solvers looks like this:

```
type Solver interface {
            Step([]ValueGrad) error
            }
```

We then have the following function that provides construction options for a `Solver`:

```
type SolverOpt func(s Solver)
```

The primary option to set is, of course, to use momentum itself; the `SolverOpt` option for this is `WithMomentum`. Solver options that apply include `WithL1Reg`, `WithL2Reg`, `WithBatchSize`, `WithClip`, and `WithLearnRate`.

Let's use our code example from the beginning of this chapter, but, instead of vanilla SGD, let's use the momentum solver in its most basic form, as follows:

```
vm := NewTapeMachine(g, BindDualValues(m.learnables()...))
solver := NewMomentum()
```

That's it! But that doesn't tell us much, just that Gorgonia is, like any good machine learning library, flexible and modular enough that we can simply swap out our solvers (and measure relative performance!).

So, let's take a look at the function we are calling, as shown in the following code:

```
func NewMomentum(opts ...SolverOpt) *Momentum {
        s := Momentum{
        eta: 0.001,
        momentum: 0.9,
        }
  for _, opt := range opts {
        opt(s)
        }
        return s
  }
```

We can see here the `momentum` constant we referenced in the original formula for this method, together with `eta`, which is our learning rate. This is all we need to do; apply the momentum solver to our model!

Nesterov momentum

In Nesterov momentum, we are changing where/when we compute the gradient. We make a big jump in the direction of the previously accumulated gradient. Then, we measure the gradient at this new position and make a correction/update accordingly.

This correction prevents the ordinary momentum algorithm from updating too quickly, hence producing fewer oscillations as the gradient descent tries to converge.

RMSprop

We can also think about optimization in a different way: what if we adjust the learning rate based on feature importance? We could decrease the learning rate when we are updating parameters on common features and then increase it when we are looking at more uncommon ones. This also means that we can spend less time optimizing the learning rate. There are several variations of this idea that have been proposed, but the most popular by far is called RMSprop.

RMSprop is a modified form of SGD that, while unpublished, is elaborated in Geoffrey Hinton's *Neural Networks for Machine Learning*. RMSprop sounds fancy, but it could just as easily be called **adaptive gradient descent**. The basic idea is you modify your learning rate based on certain conditions.

These conditions can be stated simply as follows:

- If the gradient of the function is small but consistent, then increase the learning rate
- If the gradient of the function is large but inconsistent, then decrease the learning rate

RMSprop's specific method of doing this is by dividing the learning rate for a weight by a decaying average of the previous gradients.

Gorgonia supports RMSprop natively. As with the momentum example, you simply swap out your `solver`. Here is how you define it, together with a number of `solveropts` you would want to pass in:

```
solver = NewRMSPropSolver(WithLearnRate(stepSize), WithL2Reg(l2Reg),
WithClip(clip))
```

Inspecting the underlying function, we see the following options and their associated defaults for decay factor, smoothing factor, and learning rate, respectively:

```
func NewRMSPropSolver(opts...SolverOpt) * RMSPropSolver {
    s: = RMSPropSolver {
        decay: 0.999,
        eps: 1e-8,
        eta: 0.001,
    }

        for _, ·
    opt: = range opts {
        opt(s)
    }
    return s
}
```

Summary

In this chapter, we covered how to build a simple neural network and how to inspect your graph, as well as many of the commonly used activation functions. We then covered the basics of how a neural network is trained via backpropagation and gradient descent. Finally, we discussed some of the different options for gradient descent algorithms and optimizations for your neural network.

The next chapter will cover building a practical feedforward neural network and autoencoders, as well as **Restricted Boltzmann Machines (RBMs)**.

3
Beyond Basic Neural Networks - Autoencoders and RBMs

Now that we have learned how to build and train a simple neural network, we should build some models that are suitable for real-world problems.

In this chapter, we will discuss how to build a model to recognize and generate handwriting, as well as perform collaborative filtering.

In this chapter, we will cover the following topics:

- Loading data – the **Modified National Institute of Standards and Technology** (**MNIST**) database
- Building a neural network for handwriting recognition
- Building an autoencoder – generating MNIST digits
- Building a **Restricted Boltzmann Machine** (**RBM**) for Netflix-style collaborative filtering

Loading data – MNIST

Before we can even begin to train or build our model, we first need to get some data. As it turns out, a lot of people have made data available online for us to use for this purpose. One of the best-curated datasets around is MNIST, which we will use for the first two examples in this chapter.

We'll learn how to download MNIST and load it into our Go program so that we can use it in our model.

What is MNIST?

Throughout this chapter, we're going to make use of a popular dataset called the MNIST database. This has been made available by Yann LeCun, Corinna Cortes, and Christopher Burges at `http://yann.lecun.com/exdb/mnist`.

The database gets its name from the fact that it was made by mixing two databases that contain black and white images of handwritten digits. It is an example of an ideal dataset that has been preprocessed and formatted nicely for us so that we can immediately start using it. When you download it, it is already divided into training and testing (validation) sets, with 60,000 labeled examples in the training set and 10,000 labeled examples in the test set.

Each image is exactly 28 x 28 pixels and contains a value from 1 to 255 (reflecting the pixel intensity or grayscale value). This greatly simplifies things for us, as it means that we can immediately put the image into a matrix/tensor and start training our models on it.

Loading MNIST

Gorgonia comes with an MNIST loader in its `examples` folder, and we can easily use this in our code by putting the following in our imports:

```
"gorgonia.org/gorgonia/examples/mnist"
```

Then, we can add the following lines to our code:

```
var inputs, targets tensor.Tensor
var err error
inputs, targets, err = mnist.Load("train", "./mnist/", "float64")
```

This loads our images into a tensor named `inputs` and our labels into a tensor named `targets` (given that you have uncompressed the relevant files into an `mnist` folder, which should be where your executable is running).

In this example, we are loading the training set of MNIST, so it will produce a two-dimensional tensor with a size of 60,000 x 784 for the images, and another one with a size of 60,000 x 10 for the labels. The loader in Gorgonia will also helpfully rescale all the numbers to be between 0 and 1; we like small, normalized numbers when training our models.

Building a neural network for handwriting recognition

Now that we have loaded all that useful data, let's put it to good use. Since it's full of handwritten digits, we should most certainly build a model to recognize this handwriting and what it says.

In Chapter 2, *What is a Neural Network and How Do I Train One?*, we demonstrated how to build a simple neural network. Now, it's time to build something more substantial: a model for recognizing handwriting from the MNIST database.

Introduction to the model structure

First, let's think back to the original example: we had a single-layer network, which we wanted to get from a 4 x 3 matrix to a 4 x 1 vector. Now, we have to get from an MNIST image that is 28 x 28 pixels to one single number. This number is our network's guess about which number the image actually represents.

The following screenshot represents a rough example of what we can expect to find in the MNIST data: some grayscale images of handwritten digits next to their labels (which are stored separately):

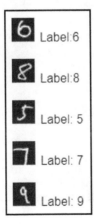

Layers

Remember that we are working with tensors, and so we need to relate this data back to those data formats. A single image can be a 28 x 28 matrix, or it can be a 784 value long vector. Our labels are currently integers from 0 to 9. However, as these are really categorical values—not a continuous numerical value from 0 to 9—it is best if we turn the results into a vector. Instead of requiring our model to produce this outright, we should think of the output as a vector of 10 values, with a 1 in the position telling us which digit it thinks it is.

This gives us the parameters that we are working with; we have to input 784 values, and then get 10 values out of our trained network. For this example, we are constructing our layers as per the following diagram:

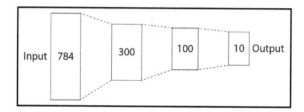

This structure would typically be described as a network with two hidden layers of **300** and **100** units each. This can be implemented in Gorgonia with the following code:

```
type nn struct {
    g *gorgonia.ExprGraph
    w0, w1, w2 *gorgonia.Node

    out *gorgonia.Node
    predVal gorgonia.Value
}

func newNN(g *gorgonia.ExprGraph) *nn {
    // Create node for w/weight
    w0 := gorgonia.NewMatrix(g, dt, gorgonia.WithShape(784, 300),
gorgonia.WithName("w0"), gorgonia.WithInit(gorgonia.GlorotN(1.0)))
    w1 := gorgonia.NewMatrix(g, dt, gorgonia.WithShape(300, 100),
gorgonia.WithName("w1"), gorgonia.WithInit(gorgonia.GlorotN(1.0)))
    w2 := gorgonia.NewMatrix(g, dt, gorgonia.WithShape(100, 10),
gorgonia.WithName("w2"), gorgonia.WithInit(gorgonia.GlorotN(1.0)))

    return &nn{
        g: g,
        w0: w0,
        w1: w1,
        w2: w2,
```

```
        }
    }
```

We are also using the ReLU activation function you learned about in Chapter 2, *What Is a Neural Network and How Do I Train One?*. As it turns out, ReLU is well suited for this task. So, a forward pass of our network looks like the following:

```
func (m *nn) fwd(x *gorgonia.Node) (err error) {
    var l0, l1, l2 *gorgonia.Node
    var l0dot, l1dot*gorgonia.Node

    // Set first layer to be copy of input
    l0 = x

    // Dot product of l0 and w0, use as input for ReLU
    if l0dot, err = gorgonia.Mul(l0, m.w0); err != nil {
        return errors.Wrap(err, "Unable to multiply l0 and w0")
    }

    // Build hidden layer out of result
    l1 = gorgonia.Must(gorgonia.Rectify(l0dot))

    // MOAR layers

    if l1dot, err = gorgonia.Mul(l1, m.w1); err != nil {
        return errors.Wrap(err, "Unable to multiply l1 and w1")
    }
    l2 = gorgonia.Must(gorgonia.Rectify(l2dot))

    var out *gorgonia.Node
    if out, err = gorgonia.Mul(l2, m.w2); err != nil {
        return errors.Wrapf(err, "Unable to multiply l2 and w2")
    }

    m.out, err = gorgonia.SoftMax(out)
    gorgonia.Read(m.out, &m.predVal)
    return
}
```

You can see that our network's final output is passed to the Gorgonia `SoftMax` function. This squashes our outputs to a sum of 1 by rescaling all the values to a value between 0 and 1. This is useful as we are using ReLU activation units, which can go into very large numbers. We want an easy way to keep our values as close as possible to our labels, which look something like the following:

```
[ 0.1 0.1 0.1 1.0 0.1 0.1 0.1 0.1 0.1 ]
```

A model trained by `SoftMax` will produce values that are like this:

```
[ 0 0 0 0.999681 0 0.000319 0 0 0 0 ]
```

By taking the element of this vector with the maximum value, we can see that the predicted label is 4.

Training

Training a model requires several important components. We have the inputs, but we also need to have a loss function and a way to interpret the outputs, as well as setting a few other hyperparameters for our model training process.

Loss functions

Loss functions play an important part in training our network. We haven't discussed them in much detail, but their role is to tell our model when it gets things wrong, so it can learn from its mistakes.

In this example, we are using a version of cross-entropy loss that has been modified to be as efficient as possible.

It should be noted that cross-entropy loss would typically be expressed in pseudocode, such as the following:

```
crossEntropyLoss = -1 * sum(actual_y * log(predicted_y))
```

However, in our case, we are going for a simpler version:

```
loss = -1 * mean(actual_y * predicted_y)
```

So, we are implementing the loss function as follows:

```
losses, err := gorgonia.HadamardProd(m.out, y)
if err != nil {
    log.Fatal(err)
}
cost := gorgonia.Must(gorgonia.Mean(losses))
cost = gorgonia.Must(gorgonia.Neg(cost))

// we wanna track costs
var costVal gorgonia.Value
gorgonia.Read(cost, &costVal)
```

As an exercise, you can modify the loss function to the more commonly used cross-entropy loss and compare your results.

Epochs, iterations, and batch sizes

As our dataset is much larger now, we need to also think about the practicalities of training it. Performing training on an item-by-item basis is fine, but we can train items in batches as well. Instead of training on all 60,000 items in MNIST, we can split up our data into 600 iterations, with batches of 100 items each. For our dataset, this means feeding our model 100 x 784 matrices as input instead of a 784-value-long vector. We could also feed it a three-dimensional tensor of 100 x 28 x 28, but we'll do that in a later chapter when we cover a model architecture that makes good use of this structure.

Since we are doing this in a programming language, we can just build a loop as follows:

```
for b := 0; b < batches; b++ {
    start := b * bs
    end := start + bs
    if start >= numExamples {
        break
    }
    if end > numExamples {
        end = numExamples
    }
}
```

And then, within each loop, we can insert our logic to extract the necessary information to feed into our machine:

```
var xVal, yVal tensor.Tensor
if xVal, err = inputs.Slice(sli{start, end}); err != nil {
    log.Fatal("Unable to slice x")
}

if yVal, err = targets.Slice(sli{start, end}); err != nil {
    log.Fatal("Unable to slice y")
}
// if err = xVal.(*tensor.Dense).Reshape(bs, 1, 28, 28); err != nil {
// log.Fatal("Unable to reshape %v", err)
// }
if err = xVal.(*tensor.Dense).Reshape(bs, 784); err != nil {
    log.Fatal("Unable to reshape %v", err)
}

gorgonia.Let(x, xVal)
gorgonia.Let(y, yVal)
```

```
if err = vm.RunAll(); err != nil {
    log.Fatalf("Failed at epoch %d: %v", i, err)
}
solver.Step(m.learnables())
vm.Reset()
```

Another term you'll hear a lot in deep learning is epochs. Epochs really just run your input data into your data multiple times. If you recall, gradient descent is an iterative process: it depends heavily on repetition to converge to the optimal solution. This means that we have a simple way to improve our model despite having only 60,000 training images: we can repeat the process a number of times until our network converges.

We can certainly manage this in several different ways. For example, we can stop repetition when the difference in our loss function between the previous epoch and the current epoch is small enough. We can also run a champion-challenger approach and take the weights from the epochs that emerge as champions on our test set. However, as we want to keep our example simple, we'll pick an arbitrary number of epochs; in this case, 100.

While we're at it, let's also add a progress bar so we can watch our model train:

```
batches := numExamples / bs
log.Printf("Batches %d", batches)
bar := pb.New(batches)
bar.SetRefreshRate(time.Second / 20)
bar.SetMaxWidth(80)

for i := 0; i < *epochs; i++ {
    // for i := 0; i < 1; i++ {
    bar.Prefix(fmt.Sprintf("Epoch %d", i))
    bar.Set(0)
    bar.Start()
    // put iteration and batch logic above here
    bar.Update()
    log.Printf("Epoch %d | cost %v", i, costVal)
}
```

Testing and validation

Training is all well and good, but we also need to know whether or not our model is actually doing what it claims to be doing. We can reuse our training code, but let's make a few changes.

First, let's remove the `solver` command. We're testing our model, not training it, so we shouldn't be updating weights:

```
solver.Step(m.learnables())
```

Second, let's actually get an image out of our dataset into a convenient file:

```
for j := 0; j < xVal.Shape()[0]; j++ {
    rowT, _ := xVal.Slice(sli{j, j + 1})
    row := rowT.Data().([]float64)

    img := visualizeRow(row)

    f, _ := os.OpenFile(fmt.Sprintf("images/%d - %d - %d - %d.jpg", b, j,
rowLabel, rowGuess), os.O_CREATE|os.O_WRONLY|os.O_TRUNC, 0644)
    jpeg.Encode(f, img, &jpeg.Options{jpeg.DefaultQuality})
    f.Close()
}
```

As you can see, the following points are true:

- b is our batch number
- j is the item number in said batch
- rowLabel is the MNIST-provided label
- rowGuess is our model's guess or prediction

Now, let's add some ways for us to extract both our data labels and our predictions into more human-readable formats (that is, as integers from 0 to 9).

For our data labels, let's add the following:

```
yRowT, _ := yVal.Slice(sli{j, j + 1})
yRow := yRowT.Data().([]float64)
var rowLabel int
var yRowHigh float64

for k := 0; k < 10; k++ {
    if k == 0 {
        rowLabel = 0
        yRowHigh = yRow[k]
    } else if yRow[k] > yRowHigh {
        rowLabel = k
        yRowHigh = yRow[k]
    }
}
```

For our predictions, we first need to extract them into a familiar format. In this case, let's put them into a tensor so we can reuse all of our earlier code:

```
arrayOutput := m.predVal.Data().([]float64)
yOutput := tensor.New(
            tensor.WithShape(bs, 10),
    tensor.WithBacking(arrayOutput)
            )
```

Notice that the output coming out of `m.predVal`, which contains our prediction values, is an array of `float64`. You can also retrieve the original shape of the object, which helps you to make a tensor of the correct shape. In this case, we know the shape already, so we'll just put those parameters straight in.

The prediction code is, of course, similar to extracting our labels from our preprocessed MNIST dataset:

```
// get prediction
predRowT, _ := yOutput.Slice(sli{j, j + 1})
predRow := predRowT.Data().([]float64)
var rowGuess int
var predRowHigh float64

// guess result
for k := 0; k < 10; k++ {
    if k == 0 {
        rowGuess = 0
        predRowHigh = predRow[k]
    } else if predRow[k] > predRowHigh {
        rowGuess = k
        predRowHigh = predRow[k]
    }
}
```

For all that hard work, you'll be rewarded with a folder full of image files with the following labels and guesses:

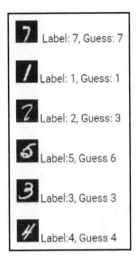

Label: 7, Guess: 7

Label: 1, Guess: 1

Label: 2, Guess: 3

Label:5, Guess 6

Label:3, Guess 3

Label:4, Guess 4

You'll see that in its current form, our model struggles with some (potentially poor) handwriting.

Taking a closer look

Alternatively, you may also want to inspect the predictions coming out, in order to get a better understanding of what's happening in your model. In that case, you may wish to extract your results into a `.csv` file, which you can do with the following code:

```
arrayOutput := m.predVal.Data().([]float64)
yOutput := tensor.New(tensor.WithShape(bs, 10),
tensor.WithBacking(arrayOutput))

file, err := os.OpenFile(fmt.Sprintf("%d.csv", b), os.O_CREATE|os.O_WRONLY,
0777)
if err = xVal.(*tensor.Dense).Reshape(bs, 784); err != nil {
  log.Fatal("Unable to create csv", err)
}
defer file.Close()
var matrixToWrite [][]string

for j := 0; j < yOutput.Shape()[0]; j++ {
  rowT, _ := yOutput.Slice(sli{j, j + 1})
  row := rowT.Data().([]float64)
  var rowToWrite []string

  for k := 0; k < 10; k++ {
      rowToWrite = append(rowToWrite, strconv.FormatFloat(row[k], 'f', 6,
```

```
64))
   }
  matrixToWrite = append(matrixToWrite, rowToWrite)
}

csvWriter := csv.NewWriter(file)
csvWriter.WriteAll(matrixToWrite)
csvWriter.Flush()
```

The output for the offending digit can be seen in the following screenshot and code output.

The following is the screenshot output:

You can also observe the same output in code:

```
[ 0   0   0.000457   0.99897   0   0   0   0.000522   0.000051   0 ]
```

Likewise, you can see it wavers from a good guess if only slightly, as shown in the following screenshot:

In code format, this is also the same:

```
[0 0 0 0 0 0 0 1 0 0]
```

Exercises

We've expanded our simple example from the Chapter 2, *What is a Neural Network and How Do I Train One?* quite a bit. At this point, it would be a good idea to have a little fun. Try the following and observe for yourself what happens, in order to get a better understanding of the impact your choices may have. For example, you should try all of the following:

- Change the loss function
- Change the number of units in each layer
- Change the number of layers
- Change the number of epochs
- Change the batch size

Building an autoencoder – generating MNIST digits

An autoencoder is exactly what it sounds like: it automatically learns how to encode data. Typically, the goal for an autoencoder is to train it to automatically encode data in fewer dimensions, or to pick out certain details or other useful things in the data. It can also be used for removing noise from the data or compressing the data.

In general, an autoencoder has two parts; an encoder half and a decoder half. We tend to train these two parts in tandem, with the goal being to get the output of the decoder to be as close as possible to our inputs.

Layers

Just like before, we need to consider our input and output. We are using MNIST again, since encoding digits is a useful feature. As such, we know that our input is 784 pixels, and we know that our output must also have 784 pixels.

Since we already have helper functions to decode our input and output into tensors, we can just leave that work aside and go straight to our neural network. Our network is as follows:

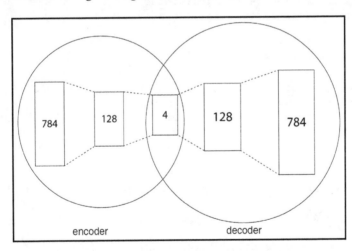

We can reuse most of our code from the last example and just change up our layers:

```
func newNN(g *gorgonia.ExprGraph) *nn {
    // Create node for w/weight
    w0 := gorgonia.NewMatrix(g, dt, gorgonia.WithShape(784, 128),
```

```
gorgonia.WithName("w0"), gorgonia.WithInit(gorgonia.GlorotU(1.0)))
    w1 := gorgonia.NewMatrix(g, dt, gorgonia.WithShape(128, 64),
gorgonia.WithName("w1"), gorgonia.WithInit(gorgonia.GlorotU(1.0)))
    w2 := gorgonia.NewMatrix(g, dt, gorgonia.WithShape(64, 128),
gorgonia.WithName("w2"), gorgonia.WithInit(gorgonia.GlorotU(1.0)))
    w3 := gorgonia.NewMatrix(g, dt, gorgonia.WithShape(128, 784),
gorgonia.WithName("w3"), gorgonia.WithInit(gorgonia.GlorotU(1.0)))

    return &nn{
        g: g,
        w0: w0,
        w1: w1,
        w2: w2,
        w3: w3,
    }
}
```

However, this time, we won't use ReLU activation functions, as we know our output has to be zeros and ones. We are using the `Sigmoid` activation function, as this gives us a convenient output. As you can see in the following code block, while we are using it for every layer, you could also just use ReLU activation functions everywhere except the last layer, since the output layer should ideally be constrained to values between 0 and 1:

```
func (m *nn) fwd(x *gorgonia.Node) (err error) {
    var l0, l1, l2, l3, l4 *gorgonia.Node
    var l0dot, l1dot, l2dot, l3dot *gorgonia.Node

    // Set first layer to be copy of input
    l0 = x

    // Dot product of l0 and w0, use as input for Sigmoid
    if l0dot, err = gorgonia.Mul(l0, m.w0); err != nil {
        return errors.Wrap(err, "Unable to multiple l0 and w0")
    }
    l1 = gorgonia.Must(gorgonia.Sigmoid(l0dot))

    if l1dot, err = gorgonia.Mul(l1, m.w1); err != nil {
        return errors.Wrap(err, "Unable to multiple l1 and w1")
    }
    l2 = gorgonia.Must(gorgonia.Sigmoid(l1dot))

    if l2dot, err = gorgonia.Mul(l2, m.w2); err != nil {
        return errors.Wrap(err, "Unable to multiple l2 and w2")
    }
    l3 = gorgonia.Must(gorgonia.Sigmoid(l2dot))

    if l3dot, err = gorgonia.Mul(l3, m.w3); err != nil {
```

```
        return errors.Wrap(err, "Unable to multiple 13 and w3")
    }
    14 = gorgonia.Must(gorgonia.Sigmoid(13dot))

    // m.pred = 13dot
    // gorgonia.Read(m.pred, &m.predVal)
    // return nil

    m.out = 14
    gorgonia.Read(14, &m.predVal)
    return

}
```

Training

As before, we need a loss function for training purposes. The input and output for an autoencoder are also different!

Loss function

This time, our loss function is different. We are using the mean of the squared errors that have pseudocode, which looks something like this:

```
mse = sum( (actual_y - predicted_y) ^ 2 ) / num_of_y
```

This can be trivially implemented in Gorgonia as follows:

```
losses, err := gorgonia.Square(gorgonia.Must(gorgonia.Sub(y, m.out)))
if err != nil {
    log.Fatal(err)
}
cost := gorgonia.Must(gorgonia.Mean(losses))
```

Input and output

Note that, this time, our input and output are the same. This means that we do not need to get the labels for our dataset and that when we are running the virtual machine, we can set both x and y to be our input data:

```
gorgonia.Let(x, xVal)
gorgonia.Let(y, xVal)
```

Epochs, iterations, and batch sizes

This problem is much harder to solve. You'll find that in order to get a feel for how our output improves, running for several epochs is very valuable here since we can write our model's output as the training takes place, with the following code:

```
for j := 0; j < 1; j++ {
    rowT, _ := yOutput.Slice(sli{j, j + 1})
    row := rowT.Data().([]float64)

    img := visualizeRow(row)

    f, _ := os.OpenFile(fmt.Sprintf("training/%d - %d - %d training.jpg",
j, b, i), os.O_CREATE|os.O_WRONLY|os.O_TRUNC, 0644)
    jpeg.Encode(f, img, &jpeg.Options{jpeg.DefaultQuality})
    f.Close()
}
```

As we're training the model, we can now watch it improve over every epoch:

You can see that we start with almost pure noise, and then very quickly get to a blurry shape, which slowly gets sharper as we progress through the epochs.

Test and validation

We won't cover the code for testing in extensive detail as we've already covered how to get our images out of our output, but note that y is now also 784 columns wide:

```
arrayOutput := m.predVal.Data().([]float64)
yOutput := tensor.New(tensor.WithShape(bs, 784),
```

```
tensor.WithBacking(arrayOutput))

for j := 0; j < yOutput.Shape()[0]; j++ {
    rowT, _ := yOutput.Slice(sli{j, j + 1})
    row := rowT.Data().([]float64)

    img := visualizeRow(row)

    f, _ := os.OpenFile(fmt.Sprintf("images/%d - %d output.jpg", b, j),
os.O_CREATE|os.O_WRONLY|os.O_TRUNC, 0644)
    jpeg.Encode(f, img, &jpeg.Options{jpeg.DefaultQuality})
    f.Close()
}
```

Now, here's the fun part; getting results out of our autoencoder:

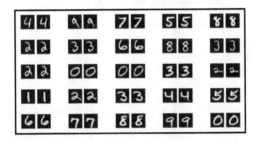

You'll notice that the results are noticeably less well defined than the input images. However, it also removes some of the noise in the images!

Building an RBM for Netflix-style collaborative filtering

We will now explore a different kind of unsupervised learning technique that, in our example, is capable of working with data that reflects a given group of users' preferences for particular pieces of content. This section will introduce new concepts around network architecture and probability distributions, as well as how they can be used in practical implementations of recommendation systems, specifically for recommending films that a given user may find interesting.

Introduction to RBMs

By their textbook definition, RBMs are **probabilistic graphical models**, which—given what we've already covered regarding the structure of neural networks—simply means a bunch of neurons that have weighted connections to another bunch of neurons.

These networks have two layers: a **visible** layer and a **hidden** layer. A visible layer is a layer into which you feed the data, and a hidden layer is a layer that isn't exposed to your data directly, but has to develop a meaningful representation of it for the task at hand. These tasks include dimensionality reduction, collaborative filtering, binary classification, and others. The restricted means that the connections are not lateral (that is, between nodes of the same layer), but rather that each hidden unit is connected to each visible unit across the layers of the network. The graph is undirected, meaning that data is not fixed into flowing in one direction. This is illustrated as follows:

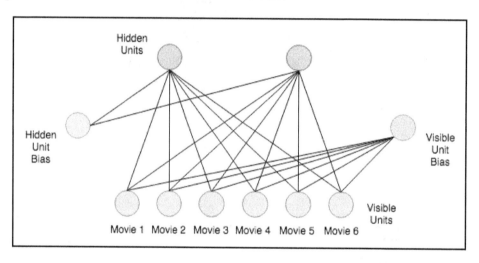

The training process is fairly straightforward and differs from our vanilla neural networks in that we are not only making a prediction, testing the strength of that prediction, and then backpropagating the error back through the network. In the case of our RBM, this is only half of the story.

To break the training process down further, a forward pass on an RBM looks like this:

- Visible layer node values are multiplied by connection weights
- A hidden unit bias is added to the sum of all nodes of the resulting value (forcing activations)
- The activation function is applied
- The value of the hidden node is given (activation probability)

Were this a deep network, the output for the hidden layer would be passed on as input to another layer. An example of this kind of architecture is a **Deep Belief Network (DBN)**, which is another important piece of work by Geoff Hinton and his group at the University of Toronto, that uses multiple RBMs stacked on top of each other.

Our RBM is not, however, a deep network. Thus, we will do something different with the hidden unit output. We will use it to attempt to reconstruct the input (visible units) of the network. We will do this by using the hidden units as input for the backward or reconstruction phase of network training.

The backward pass looks similar to the forward pass, and is performed by following these steps:

1. The activation of the hidden layer as input is multiplied by the connection weights
2. The visible unit bias is added to the sum of all nodes of the result from the multiplication
3. Calculate the reconstruction error, or the difference between the predicted input, and the actual input (known to us from our forward pass)
4. The error is used to update the weights in an effort to minimize the reconstruction error

Together, the two states (the predicted activation of the hidden layer and the predicted input of the visible layer) form a joint probability distribution.

If you're mathematically inclined, the formulas for both passes are given as follows:

- **Forward pass**: The probability of a (hidden node activation) is given a weighted input, x:

$$p(a \mid x; w)$$

- **Backward pass**: The probability of x (visible layer input) is given a weighted activation, a:

$$p(x \mid a; w)$$

- The joint probability distribution is therefore given simply by the following:

$$p(a, x)$$

Reconstruction can thus be thought of differently from the kinds of techniques we have discussed so far. It is neither regression (predicting a continuous output for a given set of inputs) nor classification (applying a class label for a given set of inputs). This is made clear by the way in which we calculate the error in the reconstruction phase. We do not merely measure input versus predicted input as a real number (a difference of the output); rather, we compare the probability distribution for all values of the x input versus all values of the *reconstructed* input. We use a method called **Kullback-Leibler divergence** to perform this comparison. Essentially, this approach measures the area under the curve of each probability distribution that does not overlap. We then try to make our weight adjustments and rerun the training loop in an attempt to reduce this divergence (error), thus bringing the curves closer together, as shown in the following diagram:

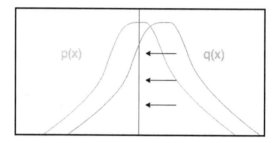

At the end of the training, when this error has been minimized, we are then able to make a prediction about what other films a given user might give the thumbs-up to.

RBMs for collaborative filtering

As discussed in the introduction to this section, RBMs can be used in a number of situations, in either a supervised or unsupervised manner. **Collaborative filtering** refers to a strategy for predicting user preferences on the underlying assumption that if user *A* likes item *Z*, and user *B* also likes item *Z*, then user *B* might also like something else that user *A* likes (say, item *Y*).

We see this use case in action every time Netflix recommends something to us or every time Amazon recommends us a new vacuum cleaner (because, of course, we bought a vacuum cleaner and are now very clearly into domestic appliances).

So now that we've covered a bit of theory on what RBMs are, how they work, and how they are used, let's jump into building one!

Preparing our data – GroupLens movie ratings

We are using the GroupLens dataset. It contains a collection of users, movies, and ratings collected from MovieLens (`http://www.movielens.org`), and is run by a number of academic researchers at the University of Minnesota.

We need to parse the `ratings.dat` file, delimited with a colon, for `userids`, `ratings`, and `movieids`. We can then match up `movieids` with those in `movies.dat`.

First, let's look at the code we need to build our index of movies:

```
package main

import (

  // "github.com/aotimme/rbm"

  "fmt"
  "log"
  "math"
  "strconv"

  "github.com/yunabe/easycsv"
  g "gorgonia.org/gorgonia"
  "gorgonia.org/tensor"
)

var datasetfilename string = "dataset/cleanratings.csv"
var movieindexfilename string = "dataset/cleanmovies.csv"

func BuildMovieIndex(input string) map[int]string {

  var entrycount int
  r := easycsv.NewReaderFile(input, easycsv.Option{
    Comma: ',',
  })

  var entry struct {
    Id int `index:"0"`
    Title string `index:"1"`
  }

  //fix hardcode
  movieindex := make(map[int]string, 3952)

  for r.Read(&entry) {
    // fmt.Println(entry)
```

```
    movieindex[entry.Id] = entry.Title
    // entries = append(entries, entry)
    entrycount++
  }

  return movieindex

}
```

Now, we write a function to import the raw data and turn it into an *m* x *n* matrix. In this, the rows represent individual users and the columns are their (normalized) ratings across every movie in our dataset:

```
func DataImport(input string) (out [][]int, uniquemovies map[int]int) {
  //
  // Initial data processing
  //
  // import from CSV, read into entries var
  r := easycsv.NewReaderFile(input, easycsv.Option{
    Comma: ',',
  })

  var entry []int
  var entries [][]int
  for r.Read(&entry) {
    entries = append(entries, entry)
  }

  // maps for if unique true/false
  seenuser := make(map[int]bool)
  seenmovie := make(map[int]bool)

  // maps for if unique index
  uniqueusers := make(map[int]int)
  uniquemovies = make(map[int]int)

  // counters for uniques
  var uniqueuserscount int = 0
  var uniquemoviescount int = 0

  // distinct movie lists/indices
  for _, e := range entries {
    if seenmovie[e[1]] == false {
      uniquemovies[uniquemoviescount] = e[1]
      seenmovie[e[1]] = true
      uniquemoviescount++
    } else if seenmovie[e[1]] == true {
      // fmt.Printf("Seen movie %v before, aborting\n", e[0])
```

```
      continue
    }
  }
  // distinct user lists/indices
  for _, e := range entries {
    if seenuser[e[0]] == false {
      uniqueusers[uniqueuserscount] = e[0]
      seenuser[e[0]] = true
      uniqueuserscount++
      // uniqueusers[e[0]] =
    } else if seenuser[e[0]] == true {
      // fmt.Printf("Seen user %v before, aborting\n", e[0])
      continue
    }
  }

  uservecs := make([][]int, len(uniqueusers))
  for i := range uservecs {
    uservecs[i] = make([]int, len(uniquemovies))
  }
```

The following is the main loop where we process each line from the CSV, and then add to the master slices of users and sub-slices of movie ratings with the correct index:

```
  var entriesloop int
  for _, e := range entries {
    // hack - wtf
    if entriesloop%100000 == 0 && entriesloop != 0 {
      fmt.Printf("Processing rating %v of %v\n", entriesloop, len(entries))
    }
    if entriesloop > 999866 {
      break
    }
    var currlike int

    // normalisze ratings
    if e[2] >= 4 {
      currlike = 1
    } else {
      currlike = 0
    }

    // add to a user's vector of index e[1]/movie num whether current movie
is +1
    // fmt.Println("Now looping uniquemovies")
    for i, v := range uniquemovies {
      if v == e[1] {
        // fmt.Println("Now setting uservec to currlike")
```

```
        // uservec[i] = currlike
        // fmt.Println("Now adding to uservecs")
        uservecs[e[0]][i] = currlike
        break
      }
    }
    // fmt.Printf("Processing rating %v of %v\n", entriesloop,
len(entries))
    entriesloop++
  }
  // fmt.Println(uservecs)
  // os.Exit(1)

  // fmt.Println(entry)
  if err := r.Done(); err != nil {
    log.Fatalf("Failed to read a CSV file: %v", err)
  }
  // fmt.Printf("length uservecs %v and uservecs.movies %v", len(uservecs))
  fmt.Println("Number of unique users: ", len(seenuser))
  fmt.Println("Number of unique movies: ", len(seenmovie))
  out = uservecs

  return

}
```

Building an RBM in Gorgonia

Now that we've cleaned up our data, created a training or test set, and written the code necessary to produce the input required by our network, we can begin coding up the RBM itself.

First, we begin with our now standard struct, the scaffold onto which we attach the various components of our network:

```
const cdS = 1
type ggRBM struct {
    g *ExprGraph
    v *Node // visible units
    vB *Node // visible unit biases - same size tensor as v
    h *Node // hidden units
    hB *Node // hidden unit biases - same size tensor as h
    w *Node // connection weights
    cdSamples int // number of samples for contrastive divergence - WHAT
ABOUT MOMENTUM
}
```

```
func (m *ggRBM) learnables() Nodes {
    return Nodes{m.w, m.vB, m.hB}
}
```

Then, we add the helper functions that attach to our RBM:

1. First, we add `func` for our `ContrastiveDivergence` learning algorithm (with Gibbs sampling):

```
// Uses Gibbs Sampling
func (r *ggRBM) ContrastiveDivergence(input *Node, learnRate
float64, k int) {
    rows := float64(r.TrainingSize)

 // CD-K
    phMeans, phSamples := r.SampleHiddenFromVisible(input)
    nvSamples := make([]float64, r.Inputs)
// iteration 0

    _, nvSamples, nhMeans, nhSamples := r.Gibbs(phSamples,
nvSamples)

    for step := 1; step < k; step++ {

        /*nvMeans*/ _, nvSamples, nhMeans, nhSamples =
r.Gibbs(nhSamples, nvSamples)

    }

    // Update weights
    for i := 0; i < r.Outputs; i++ {

        for j := 0; j < r.Inputs; j++ {

            r.Weights[i][j] += learnRate * (phMeans[i]*input[j] -
nhMeans[i]*nvSamples[j]) / rows
        }
        r.Biases[i] += learnRate * (phSamples[i] - nhMeans[i]) /
rows
    }

    // update hidden biases
    for j := 0; j < r.Inputs; j++ {

        r.VisibleBiases[j] += learnRate * (input[j] - nvSamples[j])
/ rows
    }
}
```

2. Now, we add functions to sample our respective visible or hidden layers:

```go
func (r *ggRBM) SampleHiddenFromVisible(vInput *Node) (means
[]float64, samples []float64) {
   means = make([]float64, r.Outputs)
   samples = make([]float64, r.Outputs)
   for i := 0; i < r.Outputs; i++ {
       mean := r.PropagateUp(vInput, r.Weights[i], r.Biases[i])
       samples[i] = float64(binomial(1, mean))
       means[i] = mean
   }
   return means, samples
}

func (r *ggRBM) SampleVisibleFromHidden(hInput *Node) (means
[]float64, samples []float64) {
   means = make([]float64, r.Inputs)
   samples = make([]float64, r.Inputs)
   for j := 0; j < r.Inputs; j++ {
       mean := r.PropagateDown(hInput, j, r.VisibleBiases[j])
       samples[j] = float64(binomial(1, mean))
       means[j] = mean
   }
   return means, samples
}
```

3. Next, we add a couple of functions to handle the propagation of weight updates:

```go
func (r *ggRBM) PropagateDown(h *Node, j int, hB *Node) *Node {
   retVal := 0.0
   for i := 0; i < r.Outputs; i++ {
       retVal += r.Weights[i][j] * h0[i]
   }
   retVal += bias
   return sigmoid(retVal)
}

func (r *ggRBM) PropagateUp(v *Node, w *Node, vB *Node) float64 {
   retVal := 0.0
   for j := 0; j < r.Inputs; j++ {
       retVal += weights[j] * v0[j]
   }
   retVal += bias
   return sigmoid(retVal)
}
```

4. Now, we add a function for Gibbs sampling (as used in our previous `ContrastiveDivergence` function) as well as a function to perform the reconstruction step in our network:

```go
func (r *ggRBM) Gibbs(h, v *Node) (vMeans []float64, vSamples
[]float64, hMeans []float64, hSamples []float64) {
    vMeans, vSamples = r.SampleVisibleFromHidden(r.h)
    hMeans, hSamples = r.SampleHiddenFromVisible(r.v)
    return
}

func (r *ggRBM) Reconstruct(x *Node) *Node {
    hiddenLayer := make([]float64, r.Outputs)
    retVal := make([]float64, r.Inputs)

    for i := 0; i < r.Outputs; i++ {
        hiddenLayer[i] = r.PropagateUp(x, r.Weights[i], r.Biases[i])
    }

    for j := 0; j < r.Inputs; j++ {
        activated := 0.0
        for i := 0; i < r.Outputs; i++ {
            activated += r.Weights[i][j] * hiddenLayer[i]
        }
        activated += r.VisibleBiases[j]
        retVal[j] = sigmoid(activated)
    }
    return retVal
}
```

5. After that, we add the function that instantiates our RBM:

```go
func newggRBM(g *ExprGraph, cdS int) *ggRBM {

    vT := tensor.New(tensor.WithBacking(tensor.Random(tensor.Int,
3952)), tensor.WithShape(3952, 1))

    v := NewMatrix(g,
        tensor.Int,
        WithName("v"),
        WithShape(3952, 1),
        WithValue(vT),
    )

    hT := tensor.New(tensor.WithBacking(tensor.Random(tensor.Int,
200)), tensor.WithShape(200, 1))

    h := NewMatrix(g,
```

```
        tensor.Int,
        WithName("h"),
        WithShape(200, 1),
        WithValue(hT),
    )

    wB := tensor.Random(tensor.Float64, 3952*200)
    wT := tensor.New(tensor.WithBacking(wB),
tensor.WithShape(3952*200, 1))
    w := NewMatrix(g,
        tensor.Float64,
        WithName("w"),
        WithShape(3952*200, 1),
        WithValue(wT),
    )

    return &ggRBM{
        g: g,
        v: v,
        h: h,
        w: w,
        // hB: hB,
        // vB: vB,
        cdSamples: cdS,
    }
}
```

6. Finally, we train the model:

```
func main() {
    g := NewGraph()
    m := newggRBM(g, cdS)
    data, err := ReadDataFile(datasetfilename)
    if err != nil {
        log.Fatal(err)
    }
    fmt.Println("Data read from CSV: \n", data)
    vm := NewTapeMachine(g, BindDualValues(m.learnables()...))
    // solver := NewVanillaSolver(WithLearnRate(1.0))
    for i := 0; i < 1; i++ {
        if vm.RunAll() != nil {
            log.Fatal(err)
        }
    }
}
```

Before we execute the code, we need to preprocess our data a little bit. This is because the delimiter used in our dataset is : : but we want to change it to , . The repository for this chapter includes preprocess.sh in the root of the folder, which does the following for us:

```bash
#!/bin/bash
export LC_CTYPE=C
export LANG=C
cat ratings.dat | sed 's/::/,/g' > cleanratings.csv
cat movies.dat | sed 's/,//g; s/::/,/g' > cleanmovies.csv
```

Now that we have our data formatted nicely, let's execute the code for our RBM and observe the output as follows:

```
Loading Movielens data
Building movie index
Loading and converting per-user ratings
Processing rating 100000 of 1000209
Processing rating 200000 of 1000209
Processing rating 300000 of 1000209
Processing rating 400000 of 1000209
Processing rating 500000 of 1000209
Processing rating 600000 of 1000209
Processing rating 700000 of 1000209
Processing rating 800000 of 1000209
Processing rating 900000 of 1000209
Number of unique users:   6040
Number of unique movies:   3706
3883 movies pruned to index of 3706 unique titles
Testing movie lookup:   Erin Brockovich (2000)
```

Here, we see our data import functions processing the ratings and movie index files, as well as building the per-user vectors of a length of 3706 that index all the users' ratings (normalized to 0/1):

```
Training RBM...
Training iteration: 1
Training iteration: 101
Training iteration: 201
Training iteration: 301
Training iteration: 401
Training iteration: 501
Training iteration: 601
Training iteration: 701
Training iteration: 801
Training iteration: 901
Generating sample recomendation...
3408 Grumpier Old Men (1995)
594 Tom and Huck (1995)
2398 Dracula: Dead and Loving It (1995)
2321 Money Train (1995)
745 City of Lost Children The (1995)
1022 Across the Sea of Time (1995)
1357 Lamerica (1994)
3108 Big Bully (1996)
292 Juror The (1996)
3256 Journey of August King The (1995)
```

After the training phase is complete (here, it is set at 1,000 iterations), the RBM generates a set of recommendations for a randomly selected user.

You can now experiment with the different hyperparameters and try feeding in your own data!

Summary

In this chapter, we learned about how to build a simple multilayer neural network and an autoencoder. We also explored the design and implementation of a probabilistic graphical model, the RBM, used in an unsupervised manner to create a recommendation engine for films.

It is highly recommended that you try these models and architectures on other pieces of data to see how they perform.

In the next chapter, we will have a look at the hardware side of deep learning, and also find out how exactly CPUs and GPUs serve our computational needs.

Further reading

- *Restricted Boltzmann Machines for Collaborative Filtering*, the original paper of the research group at the University of Toronto, available at `https://www.cs.toronto.edu/~rsalakhu/papers/rbmcf.pdf`
- *Restricted Boltzmann Machines Modeling Human Choice*, a paper that explores the notion that RBMs are effective at modeling *human choice* (in our example, a preference for a type of film), and suggests applications in other fields such as psychology, available at: `//papers.nips.cc/paper/5280-restricted-boltzmann-machines-modeling-human-choice.pdf`

CUDA - GPU-Accelerated Training

4

This chapter will look at the hardware side of deep learning. First, we will take a look at how CPUs and GPUs serve our computational needs for building **Deep Neural Networks** (**DNNs**), how they are different, and what their strengths are. The performance improvements offered by GPUs are central to the success of deep learning.

We will learn about how to get Gorgonia working with our GPU and how to accelerate our Gorgonia models using **CUDA**: NVIDIA's software library for facilitating the easy construction and execution of GPU-accelerated deep learning models. We will also learn about how to build a model that uses GPU-accelerated operations in Gorgonia, and then benchmark the performance of these models versus their CPU counterparts to determine which is the best option for different tasks.

In this chapter, the following topics will be covered:

- CPUs versus GPUs
- Understanding Gorgonia and CUDA
- Building a model in Gorgonia with CUDA
- Performance benchmarking of CPU versus GPU models for training and inference

CPUs versus GPUs

At this point, we've covered much of the basic theory and practice of neural networks, but we haven't given much consideration to the processors running them. So let's take a break from coding and go into more depth about the little slices of silicon that are actually doing the work.

The 30,000-foot view is that CPUs were originally designed to favor scalar operations, which are performed sequentially, and GPUs are designed for vector operations, which are performed in parallel. Neural networks perform a large number of independent calculations within a layer (say, each neuron multiplied by its weight), and so they are a processing workload amenable to a chip design that favors massive parallelism.

Let's make this a little more concrete by walking through an example of the types of operations that take advantage of the performance characteristics of each. Take the two-row vectors of [1, 2, 3] and [4, 5, 6]. If we were to perform element-wise matrix multiplication on these, it would look like this:

```
CPU, 2ns per operation (higher per-core clock than GPU, fewer cores):

1 * 4
2 * 5
3 * 6
        = [4, 10, 18]

Time taken: 6ns

GPU, 4ns per operation (lower per-core clock than CPU, more cores):

1 * 4 | 2 * 5 | 3 *6
        = [4, 10, 18]

Time taken: 4ns
```

As you can see, the CPU performed the computation sequentially, while the GPU performed it in parallel. This resulted in the GPU taking less time to complete the computation than the CPU. This is a fundamental difference between the two types of processors that we care about for the workloads associated with DNNs.

Computational workloads and chip design

How does this difference manifest in terms of the actual design of the processor itself? This diagram, taken from NVIDIA's own CUDA documentation, illustrates these differences:

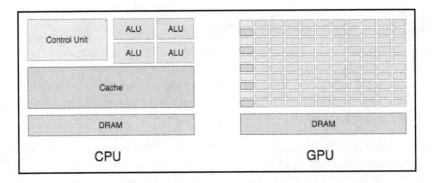

Control or cache units are reduced, while there is a significant increase in the number of cores or ALUs. This results in improvement of an order of magnitude (or more) in performance. The caveat to this is that GPU efficiency is far from perfect with respect to memory, compute, and power. This is why a number of companies are racing to design a processor for DNN workloads from the ground up, to optimize the ratio of cache units/ALUs, and to improve the way in which data is pulled into memory and then fed into the compute units. Currently, memory is a bottleneck in GPUs, as illustrated by the following diagram:

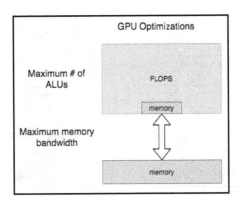

The ALUs can only work if they have something to work on. If we exhaust the on-die memory, we have to go to the L2 cache, which is faster in a GPU than in a CPU, but still takes far longer than on-die L1 memory to access. We will discuss these shortcomings in the context of new and competing chip designs in a later chapter. For now, the important thing to understand is that, ideally, we want to have as many ALUs and as much on-die cache as we can cram into a chip, in the right ratio, and with fast communication between the processors and their memory. For this process, CPUs do work, but GPUs are far better. And for now, they are the most suitable hardware for machine learning that is widely available to consumers.

Memory access in GPUs

By now, it should hopefully be clear to you that fast and local memory is key to the performance of the kinds of workloads we are offloading to our processor when doing deep learning. It is, however, not just the quantity and proximity of memory that matters, but also how this memory is accessed. Think of sequential access versus random access performance on hard drives, as the principle is the same.

Why does this matter for DNNs? Put simply, they are high-dimensional structures that have to be embedded, ultimately, in a 1D space for the memory that feeds our ALUs. Modern (vector) GPUs, built for graphics workloads, assume that they will be accessing adjacent memory, which is where one part of a 3D scene will be stored next to a related part (adjacent pixels in a frame). Thus, they are optimized for this assumption. Our networks are not 3D scenes. The layout of their data is sparse and dependent on network (and, in turn, graph) structure and the information they hold.

The following diagram represents the memory access motifs for these different workloads:

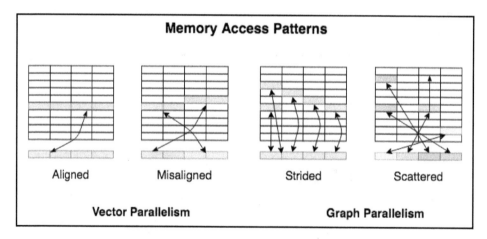

For DNNs, we are looking to get as close to **Strided** memory access patterns as possible when we write our operations. After all, matrix multiplication happens to be one of the more common operations in DNNs.

Real-world performance

To get a feel for the real-world performance differences, let's compare one of the CPUs that's best suited for neural network workloads, the Intel Xeon Phi, versus an NVIDIA Maxwell GPU from 2015.

Intel Xeon Phi CPU

Here are some hard performance numbers:

- This chip's compute units are capable of 2,400 Gflops/sec, and pulls 88 Gwords/sec from DRAM, with a ratio of 27/1
- This means that there are 27 floating-point operations per word fetched from memory

NVIDIA Maxwell GPU

Now, here are the numbers for a reference NVIDIA GPU. Pay specific attention to the change in ratio:

- 6,100 Gflops/sec
- 84 Gwords/sec
- Ratio is 72/1

So, just in terms of raw operations per chunk of memory, GPUs have a clear advantage.

A full detour into microprocessor design is of course outside the scope of this book, but it is useful to think about the processor's distribution of memory and compute units. The design philosophy for modern chips can be summed up as *cram as many floating-point units onto the chip as possible to achieve the maximum computation relative to the power required/heat generated.*

The idea is to keep those ALUs as full as possible, thus minimizing the amount of time they sit idle while memory gets filled.

Understanding Gorgonia and CUDA

Before we step into how Gorgonia works with CUDA, let's quickly introduce you to CUDA and what it is.

CUDA

CUDA is NVIDIA's programming language for its GPUs. This means your AMD card does not support CUDA. In the growing landscape of deep learning libraries, languages, and tools, it is a de facto standard. The C implementation is freely available, but of course, it is only compatible with NVIDIA's own hardware.

Basic Linear Algebra Subprograms

As we've seen in the networks we've built so far, tensor operations are fundamental to machine learning. GPUs are designed for these types of vector or matrix operations, but our software also needs to be designed to take advantage of these optimizations. Enter **BLAS**!

BLAS provide the building blocks for linear algebra operations, commonly used in graphics programming as well as machine learning. BLAS libraries are low level, originally written in Fortran, and group the functionality they offer into three *levels*, defined by the types of operations covered, as follows:

- **Level 1**: Vector operations on strided arrays, dot products, vector norms, and generalized vector addition
- **Level 2**: Generalized matrix-vector multiplication, solver for linear equations involving triangular matrices
- **Level 3**: Matrix operations, including **General Matrix Multiplication (GEMM)**

Level 3 operations are what we're really interested in for deep learning. Here's an example from the CUDA-fied convolution operation in Gorgonia.

CUDA in Gorgonia

Gorgonia has implemented support for NVIDIA's CUDA as part of its `cu` package. It abstracts out almost all the complexity, so all we have to do is simply specify the `--tags=cuda` flag at build time and ensure the operations we are calling are in fact present in the Gorgonia API.

Not every possible operation is implemented, of course. The emphasis is on operations that benefit from parallel execution, amenable to GPU acceleration. As we will cover in `Chapter 5`, *Next Word Prediction with Recurrent Neural Networks*, many of the operations involved in **Convolutional Neural Networks (CNNs)** meet this criterion.

So, what's available? The following list outlines the options:

- 1D or 2D convolutions (used in CNNs)
- 2D max pooling (also used in CNNs!)
- Dropout (kill some neurons!)
- ReLU (recall activation functions in `Chapter 2`, *What is a Neural Network and How Do I Train One?*)
- Batch normalization

We will now look at the implementation of each, in turn.

Looking at `gorgonia/ops/nn/api_cuda.go`, we see the function for a 2D convolution as follows:

```
func Conv2d(im, filter *G.Node, kernelShape tensor.Shape, pad, stride,
dilation []int) (retVal *G.Node, err error) {
    var op *convolution
    if op, err = makeConvolutionOp(im, filter, kernelShape, pad, stride,
dilation); err != nil {
        return nil, err
    }
    return G.ApplyOp(op, im, filter)
}
```

The following 1D convolution function returns an instance of `Conv2d()`, which is a neat way of providing us with both options:

```
func Conv1d(in, filter *G.Node, kernel, pad, stride, dilation int)
(*G.Node, error) {
    return Conv2d(in, filter, tensor.Shape{1, kernel}, []int{0, pad},
[]int{1, stride}, []int{1, dilation})
}
```

Next is the `MaxPool2D()` function. In a CNN, the max pooling layer is part of the process of feature extraction. The dimensionality of the input is reduced, before being passed on to the subsequent convolutional layer.

Here, we create an instance of `MaxPool` that carries our XY parameters, and we return the result of running `ApplyOp()` across our input node, as shown in the following code:

```
func MaxPool2D(x *G.Node, kernel tensor.Shape, pad, stride []int) (retVal
*G.Node, err error) {
    var op *maxpool
    if op, err = newMaxPoolOp(x, kernel, pad, stride); err != nil {
        return nil, err
    }
    return G.ApplyOp(op, x)
}
```

`Dropout()` is a regularization technique that is used to prevent our networks from overfitting. We want to learn the most general representation of our input data possible, and dropout helps us do that.

The structure of `Dropout()` should be familiar by now. It is another operation that can be parallelized within a layer, as follows:

```
func Dropout(x *G.Node, prob float64) (retVal *G.Node, err error) {
    var op *dropout
    if op, err = newDropout(x, prob); err != nil {
        return nil, err
    }

    // states := &scratchOp{x.Shape().Clone(), x.Dtype(), ""}
    // m := G.NewUniqueNode(G.WithType(x.Type()), G.WithOp(states),
G.In(x.Graph()), G.WithShape(states.shape...))

    retVal, err = G.ApplyOp(op, x)
    return
}
```

The standard ReLU function we covered in Chapter 2, *What is a Neural Network and How Do I Train One?*, is also available, as shown here:

```
func Rectify(x *G.Node) (retVal *G.Node, err error) {
  var op *activation
  if op, err = newRelu(); err != nil {
  return nil, err
  }
  retVal, err = G.ApplyOp(op, x)
  return
}
```

`BatchNorm()` is slightly more complicated. Looking back at the original paper that described batch normalization, by Szegedy and Ioffe (2015), we see how, for a given batch, we normalize the output of the previous layer by subtracting the mean of the batch and dividing by the standard deviation. We can also observe the addition of two parameters that we will train with SGD.

And now, we can see the CUDA-fied Gorgonia implementation as follows. First, let's perform the function definition and a data type check:

```
func BatchNorm(x, scale, bias *G.Node, momentum, epsilon float64) (retVal,
  γ, β *G.Node, op *BatchNormOp, err error) {
    dt, err := dtypeOf(x.Type())
    if err != nil {
        return nil, nil, nil, nil, err
    }
```

Then, it needs to create some scratch variables to allow the VM to allocate spare memory:

```
channels := x.Shape()[1]
H, W := x.Shape()[2], x.Shape()[3]
scratchShape := tensor.Shape{1, channels, H, W}

meanScratch := &gpuScratchOp{scratchOp{x.Shape().Clone(), dt, "mean"}}
varianceScratch := &gpuScratchOp{scratchOp{x.Shape().Clone(), dt,
"variance"}}
cacheMeanScratch := &gpuScratchOp{scratchOp{scratchShape, dt, "cacheMean"}}
cacheVarianceScratch := &gpuScratchOp{scratchOp{scratchShape, dt,
"cacheVariance"}}
```

We then create the equivalent variables in our computation graph:

```
g := x.Graph()

dims := len(x.Shape())

mean := G.NewTensor(g, dt, dims, G.WithShape(scratchShape.Clone()...),
G.WithName(x.Name()+"_mean"), G.WithOp(meanScratch))

variance := G.NewTensor(g, dt, dims, G.WithShape(scratchShape.Clone()...),
G.WithName(x.Name()+"_variance"), G.WithOp(varianceScratch))

cacheMean := G.NewTensor(g, dt, dims, G.WithShape(scratchShape.Clone()...),
G.WithOp(cacheMeanScratch))

cacheVariance := G.NewTensor(g, dt, dims,
G.WithShape(scratchShape.Clone()...), G.WithOp(cacheVarianceScratch))
```

We then create our scale and bias variables in the graph, before applying our function and returning the results:

```
if scale == nil {
    scale = G.NewTensor(g, dt, dims, G.WithShape(scratchShape.Clone()...),
G.WithName(x.Name()+"_γ"), G.WithInit(G.GlorotN(1.0)))
}

if bias == nil {
    bias = G.NewTensor(g, dt, dims, G.WithShape(scratchShape.Clone()...),
G.WithName(x.Name()+"_β"), G.WithInit(G.GlorotN(1.0)))
}

op = newBatchNormOp(momentum, epsilon)

retVal, err = G.ApplyOp(op, x, scale, bias, mean, variance, cacheMean,
cacheVariance)
```

```
return retVal, scale, bias, op, err
```

Next, let's take a look at how to build a model in Gorgonia that leverages CUDA.

Building a model in Gorgonia with CUDA support

Building a model in Gorgonia with CUDA support that we do a few things first. We need to install Gorgonia's cu interface to CUDA, and then have a model ready to train!

Installing CUDA support for Gorgonia

To make use of CUDA, you need a computer with a GPU made by NVIDIA. Unfortunately, setting up CUDA to work with Gorgonia is a slightly more involved process, as it involves setting up a C compiler environment to work with Go, as well as a C compiler environment that works with CUDA. NVIDIA has kindly ensured that its compiler works with the common toolchain for each platform: Visual Studio on Windows, Clang-LLVM on macOS, and GCC on Linux.

Installing CUDA and ensuring that everything works correctly requires a fair bit of work. We'll look at doing this for Windows and Linux. As Apple has not made a computer featuring an NVIDIA GPU for several years (as of writing this), we will not cover how to do this on macOS. You can still use CUDA by connecting an external GPU to your macOS, but this is a fairly involved process and Apple does not (as of writing this) have an officially supported setup with an NVIDIA GPU.

Linux

As we've discussed, once CUDA is set up nicely, running your Gorgonia code on your GPU is as simple as adding -tags=cuda when building it. But how do we get to a point where that is possible? Let's find out.

This guide requires you to install standard Ubuntu 18.04. NVIDIA provides distribution-independent instructions (and troubleshooting steps) at: https://docs.nvidia.com/cuda/cuda-installation-guide-linux/index.html.

At a high level, you need to install the following packages:

- NVIDIA driver
- CUDA
- cuDNN
- libcupti-dev

First, you need to ensure you have NVIDIA's proprietary (not the open source default) driver installed. A quick way to check whether you are running it is to execute `nvidia-smi`. You should see output similar to the following, which indicates the driver version number and other details about your GPU:

```
> nvidia-smi
Sun Jul 15 09:57:05 2018
+------------------------------------------------------------+
| NVIDIA-SMI 390.59                   Driver Version: 390.59 |
|-------------------------------+--------------------+-------+
| GPU   Name         Persistence-M| Bus-Id        Disp.A | Vol |
```

If you get `command not found`, you have a couple of options, depending on the distribution of Linux you are running. The latest Ubuntu distribution allows you to install most of CUDA's dependencies (including the proprietary NVIDIA driver) from the default repositories. This can be done by executing the following:

```
sudo apt install nvidia-390 nvidia-cuda-toolkit libcupti-dev
```

Alternatively, you can follow the steps in the official NVIDIA guide (linked previously) to manually install the various dependencies.

Once the installation has completed and you have rebooted your system, confirm that the drivers are installed by running `nvidia-smi` again. You also need to verify that the CUDA C compiler (part of the `nvidia-cuda-toolkit` package) is installed by executing `nvcc --version`. The output should look similar to the following:

```
> nvcc --version
nvcc: NVIDIA (R) Cuda compiler driver
Copyright (c) 2005-2017 NVIDIA Corporation
Built on Fri_Nov__3_21:07:56_CDT_2017
Cuda compilation tools, release 9.1, V9.1.85
```

Once CUDA itself is installed, there are some additional steps you need to perform to ensure that Gorgonia has the necessary CUDA libraries compiled and available for use:

1. Ensure that the target directory for the modules you are building exists. If not, create it with the following command:

   ```
   mkdir $GOPATH/src/gorgonia.org/gorgonia/cuda\ modules/target
   ```

2. Run cudagen to build the modules as follows:

   ```
   cd $GOPATH/src/gorgonia.org/gorgonia/cmd/cudagen
   go run main.go
   ```

3. After the program executes, verify that the /target directory is populated with files representing CUDA-fied operations that we will use when building our networks, as shown in the following screenshot:

   ```
   Jul  9 21:34 elembinop.ptx
   Jul  9 21:34 elemunaryop.ptx
   Jul  9 21:34 sigmoid32.ptx
   Jul  9 21:34 sigmoid64.ptx
   ```

4. Now that the preliminaries are out of the way, let's test that everything is working using the following commands:

   ```
   go install gorgonia.org/cu/cmd/cudatest cudatest
   cd $GOPATH/src/gorgonia.org/cu/cmd/cudatest
   go run main.go
   ```

You should see output similar to the following:

```
> go run main.go
CUDA version: 9010
CUDA devices: 1
Device 0

========
Name        :     "GeForce GTX 1060 6GB"
Clock Rate:       1784500 kHz
Memory      :     6370295808 bytes
Compute     :     6.1
```

You're now ready to take advantage of all the computing capacity provided by your GPU!

Windows

The setup for Windows is very similar, but you also need to provide the C compilers that are required for both Go and CUDA. This setup is outlined in the following steps:

1. Install a GCC environment; the easiest way to do this on Windows is to install MSYS2. You can download MSYS2 from `https://www.msys2.org/`.

2. After installing MSYS2, update your installation with the following commands:

   ```
   pacman -Syu
   ```

3. Restart MSYS2 and run the following again:

   ```
   pacman -Su
   ```

4. Install the GCC package as follows:

   ```
   pacman -S mingw-w64-x86_64-toolchain
   ```

5. Install Visual Studio 2017 to get a compiler compatible with CUDA. At the time of writing, you can download this from `https://visualstudio.microsoft.com/downloads/`. The Community Edition works fine; if you have a license for any of the other editions, they will do as well.

6. Install CUDA. Download this from the NVIDIA website at: `https://developer.nvidia.com/cuda-downloads`. In my experience, the network installer is less reliable than the local installer, so do try the local installer if you cannot get the network installer to work.

7. Following that, you should also install cuDNN from NVIDIA: `https://developer.nvidia.com/cudnn`. The installation process is literally a copy and paste operation and is fairly straightforward.

8. Set up the environment variables so that Go and the NVIDIA CUDA compiler driver (`nvcc`) know where to find the relevant compilers. You should replace paths, where appropriate, with the location where CUDA, MSYS2, and Visual Studio are installed. The items you need to add and the relevant variable names are as follows:

   ```
   C_INCLUDE_PATH
   C:\Program Files\NVIDIA GPU Computing Toolkit\CUDA\v9.2\include

   LIBRARY_PATH
   C:\Program Files\NVIDIA GPU Computing Toolkit\CUDA\v9.2\lib\x64

   PATH
   C:\Program Files\NVIDIA GPU Computing Toolkit\CUDA\v9.2\bin
   ```

```
C:\Program Files\NVIDIA GPU Computing Toolkit\CUDA\v9.2\libnvvp
C:\msys64\mingw64\bin
C:\Program Files (x86)\Microsoft Visual Studio
14.0\VC\bin\x86_amd64
```

9. Your environment should now be set up correctly to compile CUDA-enabled Go binaries.

Now, for Gorgonia, you need to do a few things first, as outlined in the following steps:

1. Firstly, ensure the following `target` directory for the modules you will be building exists:

   ```
   $GOPATH/src/gorgonia.org/gorgonia/cuda\ modules/target
   ```

2. Next, run `cudagen` to build the modules as follows:

   ```
   cd $GOPATH/src/gorgonia.org/gorgonia/cmd/cudagen
   go run main.go
   ```

3. Now that you have everything in place, you should install `cudatest`, like so:

   ```
   go install gorgonia.org/cu/cmd/cudatest cudatest
   ```

4. If you run `cudatest` now and all is well, you will get something similar to the following output:

   ```
   CUDA version: 9020
   CUDA devices: 1
   Device 0
   ========
   Name : "GeForce GTX 1080"
   Clock Rate: 1835000 kHz
   Memory : 8589934592 bytes
   Compute : 6.1
   ```

Performance benchmarking of CPU versus GPU models for training and inference

Now that we've done all that work, let's explore some of the advantages of using a GPU for deep learning. First, let's go through how to actually get your application to use CUDA, and then we'll go through some of the CPU and GPU speeds.

How to use CUDA

If you've completed all the previous steps to get CUDA working, then using CUDA is a fairly simple affair. You simply need to compile your application with the following:

```
go build -tags='cuda'
```

This builds your executable with CUDA support and uses CUDA, rather than the CPU, to run your deep learning model.

To illustrate, let's use an example we're already familiar with – a neural network with weights:

```
w0 := gorgonia.NewMatrix(g, dt, gorgonia.WithShape(784, 300),
gorgonia.WithName("w0"), gorgonia.WithInit(gorgonia.GlorotN(1.0)))

w1 := gorgonia.NewMatrix(g, dt, gorgonia.WithShape(300, 100),
gorgonia.WithName("w1"), gorgonia.WithInit(gorgonia.GlorotN(1.0)))

w2 := gorgonia.NewMatrix(g, dt, gorgonia.WithShape(100, 10),
gorgonia.WithName("w2"), gorgonia.WithInit(gorgonia.GlorotN(1.0)))
```

This is just our simple feedforward neural network that we built to use on the MNIST dataset.

CPU results

By running the code, we get output telling us when we started each epoch, and roughly what our cost function value was for the last execution. For this specific task, we're only running it for 10 epochs and the results can be seen as follows:

```
2018/07/21 23:48:45 Batches 600
2018/07/21 23:49:12 Epoch 0 | cost -0.6898460176511779
2018/07/21 23:49:38 Epoch 1 | cost -0.6901109698353116
2018/07/21 23:50:05 Epoch 2 | cost -0.6901978951202982
2018/07/21 23:50:32 Epoch 3 | cost -0.6902410983814113
2018/07/21 23:50:58 Epoch 4 | cost -0.6902669350941992
2018/07/21 23:51:25 Epoch 5 | cost -0.6902841232197489
2018/07/21 23:51:52 Epoch 6 | cost -0.6902963825164774
2018/07/21 23:52:19 Epoch 7 | cost -0.6903055672849466
2018/07/21 23:52:46 Epoch 8 | cost -0.6903127053988457
2018/07/21 23:53:13 Epoch 9 | cost -0.690318412509433
2018/07/21 23:53:13 Run Tests
2018/07/21 23:53:19 Epoch Test | cost -0.6887220522190024
```

We can see that every epoch takes around 26–27 seconds on this CPU, an Intel Core i7-2700K.

GPU results

We can do the same for the GPU build of the executable. This allows us to compare how long an epoch takes to train through the model. As our model is not complex, we don't expect to see that much of a difference:

```
2018/07/21 23:54:31 Using CUDA build
2018/07/21 23:54:32 Batches 600
2018/07/21 23:54:56 Epoch 0 | cost -0.6914807096357707
2018/07/21 23:55:19 Epoch 1 | cost -0.6917470871356043
2018/07/21 23:55:42 Epoch 2 | cost -0.6918343739257966
2018/07/21 23:56:05 Epoch 3 | cost -0.6918777292080605
2018/07/21 23:56:29 Epoch 4 | cost -0.6919036464362168
2018/07/21 23:56:52 Epoch 5 | cost -0.69192088335746
2018/07/21 23:57:15 Epoch 6 | cost -0.6919331749749763
2018/07/21 23:57:39 Epoch 7 | cost -0.691942382545885
2018/07/21 23:58:02 Epoch 8 | cost -0.6919495375223687
2018/07/21 23:58:26 Epoch 9 | cost -0.691955257565567
2018/07/21 23:58:26 Run Tests
2018/07/21 23:58:32 Epoch Test | cost -0.6896057773382677
```

On this GPU (an NVIDIA Geforce GTX960), we can see that this is marginally faster for this simple task, at 23–24 seconds.

Summary

In this chapter, we had a look at the hardware side of deep learning. We also had a look at how CPUs and GPUs serve our computational needs. We also looked at how CUDA, NVIDIA's software, facilitates GPU-accelerated deep learning that is implemented in Gorgonia, and finally, we looked at how to build a model that uses the features implemented by CUDA Gorgonia.

In the next chapter, we will look into vanilla RNNs and the issues involved with RNNs. We will also learn about how to build an LSTM in Gorgonia as well.

Section 2: Implementing Deep Neural Network Architectures

2

The objective of this section is to give the reader an understanding of how to implement Deep Neural Network architectures.

The following chapters are included in this section:

5
Next Word Prediction with Recurrent Neural Networks

So far, we've covered a number of basic neural network architectures and their learning algorithms. These are the necessary building blocks for designing networks that are capable of more advanced tasks, such as machine translation, speech recognition, time series prediction, and image segmentation. In this chapter, we'll cover a class of algorithms/architectures that excel at these and other tasks due to their ability to model sequential dependencies in the data.

These algorithms have proven to be incredibly powerful, and their variants have found wide application in industry and consumer use cases. This runs the gamut of machine translation, text generation, named entity recognition, and sensor data analysis. When you say *Okay, Google!* or *Hey, Siri!*, behind the scenes, a type of trained **recurrent neural network** (**RNN**) is doing inference. The common theme of all of these applications is that these sequences (such as sensor data at time x, or occurrence of a word in a corpus at position y) can all be modeled with *time* as their regulating dimension. As we will see, we can represent our data and structure our tensors accordingly.

A great example of a hard problem is natural language processing and comprehension. If we have a large body of text, say the collected works of Shakespeare, what might we be able to say about this text? We could elaborate on the statistical properties of the text, that is, how many words there are, how many of these words are unique, the total number of characters, and so on, but we also inherently know from our own experience of reading that an important property of text/language is **sequence**; that is, the order in which words appear. That order contributes to our understanding of syntax and grammar, not to mention meaning itself. It is when analyzing this kind of data that the networks we've covered so far fall short.

In this chapter, we will learn about the following topics:

- What is a basic RNN
- How to train RNNs
- Improvements of the RNN architecture, including **Gated Recurrent Unit (GRU)/Long Short-Term Memory (LSTM)** networks
- How to implement an RNN with LSTM units in Gorgonia

Vanilla RNNs

According to their more utopian description, RNNs are able to do something that the networks we've covered so far cannot: remember. More precisely, in a simple network with a single hidden layer, the network's output, as well as the state of that hidden layer, are combined with the next element in a training sequence to form the input for a new network (with its own trainable, hidden state). A *vanilla* RNN can be visualized as follows:

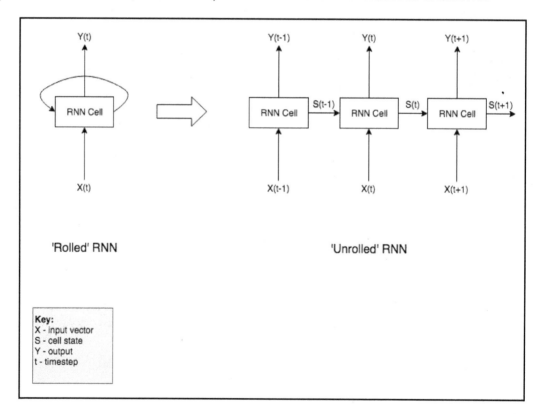

Let's unpack this a bit. The two networks in the preceding diagram are two different representations of the same thing. One is in a **Rolled** state, which is simply an abstract representation of the computation graph, where an infinite number of timesteps is represented by **(t)**. We then use the **Unrolled RNN** as we feed the network data and train it.

For a given forward pass, this network takes two inputs, where **X** is a representation of a piece of training data, and a previous *hidden* state **S** (initialized at **t0** as a vector of zeros) and a timestep **t** (the position in the sequence) repeats operations (vector concatenation of the inputs, that is, `Sigmoid` activation) on the products of these inputs and their trainable parameters. We then apply our learning algorithm, a slight twist on backpropagation, which we will cover next, and thus have the basic model of what an RNN is, what it's made of, and how it works.

Training RNNs

The way we train these networks is by using **backpropagation through time** (**BPTT**). This is an exotic name for a slight variation of something you already know of from `Chapter 2`, *What is a Neural Network and How Do I Train One?*. In this section, we will explore this variation in detail.

Backpropagation through time

With RNNs, we have multiple copies of the same network, one for each timestep. Therefore, we need a way to backpropagate the error derivatives and calculate weight updates for each of the parameters in every timestep. The way we do this is simple. We're following the contours of a function so that we can try and optimize its shape. We have multiple copies of the trainable parameters, one at each timestep, and we want these copies to be consistent with each other so that when we calculate all the gradients for a given parameter, we take their average. We use this to update the parameter at *t0* for each iteration of the learning process.

The goal is to calculate the error as that accumulates across timesteps, and unroll/roll the network and update the weights accordingly. There is, of course, a computational cost to this; that is, the amount of computation required increases with the number of timesteps. The method for dealing with this is to *truncate* (hence, *truncated BPTT*) the sequence of input/output pairs, meaning that we only roll/unroll a sequence of 20 timesteps at once, making the problem tractable.

Additional information for those who are interested in exploring the math behind this can be found in the *Further reading* section of this chapter.

Cost function

The cost function that we use with RNNs is cross-entropy loss. There is nothing special about its implementation for RNNs versus a simple binary classification task. Here, we are comparing the two probability distributions—one predicted, one expected. We calculate the error at each time step and sum them.

RNNs and vanishing gradients

RNNs themselves are an important architectural innovation, but run into problems in terms of their gradients *vanishing*. When gradient values become so small that the updates are equally tiny, this slows or even halts learning. Your digital neurons die, and your network doesn't do what you want it to do. But is a neural network with a bad memory better than one with no memory at all?

Let's zoom in a bit and discuss what's actually going on when you run into this problem. Recall the formula for calculating the value for a given weight during backpropagation:

$$W = W - LR*G$$

Here, the weight value equals the weight minus (learning rate multiplied by the gradient).

Your network is propagating error derivatives across layers and across timesteps. The larger your dataset, the greater the number of timesteps and parameters, and so the greater the number of layers. At each step, the unrolled RNN contains an activation function that squashes the output of the network to be between 0 and 1.

The repetition of these operations on gradient values that are very close to zero means that neurons *die*, or cease to *fire*. The mathematical representation on our computation graph of the neuronal model becomes brittle. This is because if the changes in the parameter we are learning about are too small to have an effect on the output of the network itself, then the network will fail to learn the value for that parameter.

So, instead of using the entirety of the hidden state from the previous timestep, is there another way to make the network a bit smarter in terms of what information it chooses to keep as we step our network through time during the training process? The answer is yes! Let's consider these changes to the network architecture.

Augmenting your RNN with GRU/LSTM units

So, what if you wanted to build a machine that writes like a dead author? Or understands that a pop in the price of a stock two weeks ago might mean that the stock will pop again today? For sequence prediction tasks where key information is observed early on in training, say at *t+1*, but necessary to make an accurate prediction at *t+250*, vanilla RNNs struggle. This is where LSTM (and, for some tasks, GRU) networks come into the picture. Instead of a simple cell, you have multiple, conditional *mini* neural networks, each determining whether or not to carry information across timesteps. We will now discuss each of these variations in detail.

Long Short-Term Memory units

Special thanks to the group of Swiss researchers who published a paper titled *Long Short-Term Memory* in 1997, which described a method for further augmenting RNNs with a more advanced *memory*.

So, what does *memory* in this context actually mean? LSTMs take the *dumb* RNN cell and add another neural network (consisting of inputs, operations, and activations), which will be selective about what information is carried from one timestep to another. It does this by maintaining a *cell state* (like a vanilla RNN cell) and a new hidden state, both of which are then fed into the next step. These *gates*, as indicated in the following diagram, learn about what information should be maintained in the hidden state:

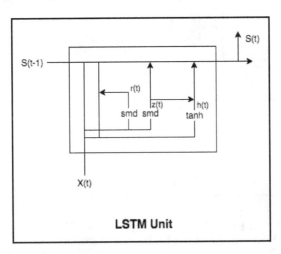

LSTM Unit

Here, we can see that multiple gates are contained within **r(t)**, **z(t)**, and **h(t)**. Each has an activation function: Sigmoid for **r** and **z** and **tanh** for **h(t)**.

Gated Recurrent Units

An alternative to LSTM units are GRUs. These were first described by a team that was led by another significant figure in the history of deep learning, Yoshua Bengio. Their initial paper, *Learning Phrase Representations using RNN Encoder–Decoder for Statistical Machine Translation* (2014), offers an interesting way of thinking about these ways of augmenting the effectiveness of our RNNs.

Specifically, they draw an equivalence between the `Tanh` activation function in a vanilla RNN and LSTM/GRU units, also describing them as *activations*. The difference in the nature of their activation is whether information is retained, unchanged, or updated in the units themselves. In effect, the use of the `Tanh` function means that your network becomes even more selective about the information that takes it from one step to the next.

GRUs differ from LSTMs in that they get rid of the *cell state*, thus reducing the overall number of tensor operations your network is performing. They also use a single reset gate instead of the LSTM's input and forget gates, further simplifying the network's architecture.

Here is a logical representation of the GRU:

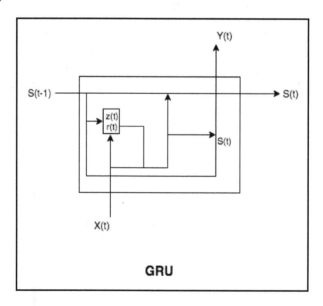

GRU

Here, we can see a combination of the forget/input gates in a single reset gate (**z(t)** and **r(t)**), with the single state **S(t)** carried forward to the next timestep.

Bias initialization of gates

Recently, at an ML conference, the *International Conference on Learning Representations*, a paper was delivered by a team from Facebook AI Research that described the progress of RNNs. This paper was concerned with the effectiveness of RNNs that had been augmented with GRU/LSTM units. Though a deep dive into the paper is outside the scope of this book, you can read more about it in the *Further reading* section, at the end of this chapter. An interesting hypothesis fell out of their research: that these units could have their bias vector initialized in a certain way, and that this would improve the network's ability to learn very long-term dependencies. They published their results, and it was shown that there seems to be an improvement in the training time and the speed with which perplexity is reduced:

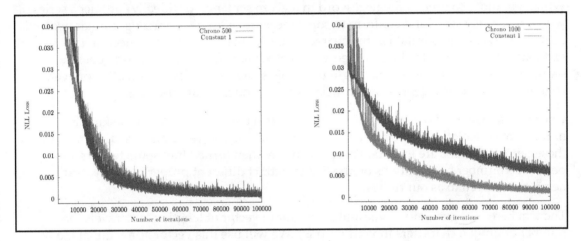

This graph, taken from the paper, represents the network's loss on the y axis, and the number of training iterations on the x axis. The red indicates *chrono initialization*.

This is very new research, and there is definite scientific value in understanding why LSTM/GRU-based networks perform as well as they do. The main practical implications of this paper, namely the initialization of the gated unit's biases, offer us yet another tool to improve model performance and save those precious GPU cycles. For now, these performance improvements are the most significant (though still incremental) on the word-level PTB and character-level text8 datasets. The network we will build in the next section can be easily adapted to test out the relative performance improvements of this change.

Building an LSTM in Gorgonia

Now that we've discussed what RNNs are, how to train them, and how to modify them for improved performance, let's build one! The next few sections will cover how we process and represent data for an RNN that uses LSTM units. We will also look at what the network itself looks like, the code for GRU units, and some tools for understanding what our network is doing, too.

Representing text data

While our aim is to predict the next word in a given sentence, or (ideally) predict a series of words that make sense and conform to some measure of English syntax/grammar, we will actually be encoding our data at the character level. This means that we need to take our text data (in this example, the collected works of William Shakespeare) and generate a sequence of tokens. These tokens might be whole sentences, individual words, or even characters themselves, depending on what type of model we are training.

Once we've tokenized out text data, we need to turn these tokens into some kind of numeric representation that's amenable to computation. As we've discussed, in our case, these representations are tensors. These tokens are then turned into some tensors and perform a number of operations on the text to extract different properties of the text, hereafter referred to as our *corpus*.

The aim here is to generator a vocabulary vector (a vector of length n, where n is the number of unique characters in your corpus). We will use this vector as a template to encode each character.

Importing and processing input

Let's start by creating a `vocab.go` file in the root of our project directory. In here, you will define a number of reserved unicode characters that will represent the beginning/end of our sequences, as well as a `BLANK` character for padding out our sequences.

Note that we do not include our `shakespeare.txt` input file here. Instead, we build a vocabulary and index, and split up our input `corpus` into chunks:

```
package main

import (
  "fmt"
  "strings"
```

```
)

const START rune = 0x02
const END rune = 0x03
const BLANK rune = 0x04

// vocab related
var sentences []string
var vocab []rune
var vocabIndex map[rune]int
var maxsent int = 30

func initVocab(ss []string, thresh int) {
  s := strings.Join(ss, " ")
  fmt.Println(s)
  dict := make(map[rune]int)
  for _, r := range s {
    dict[r]++
  }

  vocab = append(vocab, START)
  vocab = append(vocab, END)
  vocab = append(vocab, BLANK)
  vocabIndex = make(map[rune]int)

  for ch, c := range dict {
    if c >= thresh {
      // then add letter to vocab
      vocab = append(vocab, ch)
    }
  }

  for i, v := range vocab {
    vocabIndex[v] = i
  }

  fmt.Println("Vocab: ", vocab)
  inputSize = len(vocab)
  outputSize = len(vocab)
  epochSize = len(ss)
  fmt.Println("\ninputs :", inputSize)
  fmt.Println("\noutputs :", outputSize)
  fmt.Println("\nepochs: :", epochSize)
  fmt.Println("\nmaxsent: :", maxsent)
}

func init() {
  sentencesRaw := strings.Split(corpus, "\n")
```

```
    for _, s := range sentencesRaw {
      s2 := strings.TrimSpace(s)
      if s2 != "" {
        sentences = append(sentences, s2)
      }

    }

    initVocab(sentences, 1)
  }
```

We can now create the next chunk of code, which provides us with helper functions that we will need later on. More specifically, we will add two sampling functions: one is temperature-based, where the probability of already-high probability words is increased, and decreased in the case of low-probability words. The higher the temperature, the greater the probability bump in either direction. This gives you another tunable feature in your LSTM-RNN.

Lastly, we will include some functions to work with `byte` and `uint` slices, allowing you to easily compare/swap/evaluate them:

```go
package main

import (
  "math/rand"

  "gorgonia.org/gorgonia"
  "gorgonia.org/tensor"
)

func sampleT(val gorgonia.Value) int {
  var t tensor.Tensor
  var ok bool
  if t, ok = val.(tensor.Tensor); !ok {
    panic("Expects a tensor")
  }

  return tensor.SampleIndex(t)
}

func sample(val gorgonia.Value) int {

  var t tensor.Tensor
  var ok bool
  if t, ok = val.(tensor.Tensor); !ok {
    panic("expects a tensor")
  }
```

```
  indT, err := tensor.Argmax(t, -1)
  if err != nil {
    panic(err)
  }
  if !indT.IsScalar() {
    panic("Expected scalar index")
  }
  return indT.ScalarValue().(int)
}

func shuffle(a []string) {
  for i := len(a) - 1; i > 0; i-- {
    j := rand.Intn(i + 1)
    a[i], a[j] = a[j], a[i]
  }
}

type byteslice []byte

func (s byteslice) Len() int { return len(s) }
func (s byteslice) Less(i, j int) bool { return s[i] < s[j] }
func (s byteslice) Swap(i, j int) { s[i], s[j] = s[j], s[i] }

type uintslice []uint

func (s uintslice) Len() int { return len(s) }
func (s uintslice) Less(i, j int) bool { return s[i] < s[j] }
func (s uintslice) Swap(i, j int) { s[i], s[j] = s[j], s[i] }
```

Next, we will create an lstm.go file, where we will define our LSTM units. They will look like little neural networks, because as we've discussed previously, that's what they are. The input, forget, and output gates will be defined, along with their associated weights/biases.

The MakeLSTM() function will add these units to our graph. The LSTM has a number of methods too; that is, learnables() is used for producing our learnable parameters, and Activate() is used to define the operations our units perform when processing input data:

```
package main

import (
  . "gorgonia.org/gorgonia"
)

type LSTM struct {
  wix *Node
  wih *Node
```

```go
    bias_i *Node

    wfx *Node
    wfh *Node
    bias_f *Node

    wox *Node
    woh *Node
    bias_o *Node

    wcx *Node
    wch *Node
    bias_c *Node
}

func MakeLSTM(g *ExprGraph, hiddenSize, prevSize int) LSTM {
    retVal := LSTM{}

    retVal.wix = NewMatrix(g, Float, WithShape(hiddenSize, prevSize),
WithInit(GlorotN(1.0)), WithName("wix_"))
    retVal.wih = NewMatrix(g, Float, WithShape(hiddenSize, hiddenSize),
WithInit(GlorotN(1.0)), WithName("wih_"))
    retVal.bias_i = NewVector(g, Float, WithShape(hiddenSize),
WithName("bias_i_"), WithInit(Zeroes()))

    // output gate weights

    retVal.wox = NewMatrix(g, Float, WithShape(hiddenSize, prevSize),
WithInit(GlorotN(1.0)), WithName("wfx_"))
    retVal.woh = NewMatrix(g, Float, WithShape(hiddenSize, hiddenSize),
WithInit(GlorotN(1.0)), WithName("wfh_"))
    retVal.bias_o = NewVector(g, Float, WithShape(hiddenSize),
WithName("bias_f_"), WithInit(Zeroes()))

    // forget gate weights

    retVal.wfx = NewMatrix(g, Float, WithShape(hiddenSize, prevSize),
WithInit(GlorotN(1.0)), WithName("wox_"))
    retVal.wfh = NewMatrix(g, Float, WithShape(hiddenSize, hiddenSize),
WithInit(GlorotN(1.0)), WithName("woh_"))
    retVal.bias_f = NewVector(g, Float, WithShape(hiddenSize),
WithName("bias_o_"), WithInit(Zeroes()))

    // cell write

    retVal.wcx = NewMatrix(g, Float, WithShape(hiddenSize, prevSize),
WithInit(GlorotN(1.0)), WithName("wcx_"))
    retVal.wch = NewMatrix(g, Float, WithShape(hiddenSize, hiddenSize),
```

```
WithInit(GlorotN(1.0)), WithName("wch_"))
  retVal.bias_c = NewVector(g, Float, WithShape(hiddenSize),
WithName("bias_c_"), WithInit(Zeroes()))
  return retVal
}

func (l *LSTM) learnables() Nodes {
  return Nodes{
    l.wix, l.wih, l.bias_i,
    l.wfx, l.wfh, l.bias_f,
    l.wcx, l.wch, l.bias_c,
    l.wox, l.woh, l.bias_o,
  }
}

func (l *LSTM) Activate(inputVector *Node, prev lstmout) (out lstmout, err
error) {
  // log.Printf("prev %v", prev.hidden.Shape())
  prevHidden := prev.hidden
  prevCell := prev.cell
  var h0, h1, inputGate *Node
  h0 = Must(Mul(l.wix, inputVector))
  h1 = Must(Mul(l.wih, prevHidden))
  inputGate = Must(Sigmoid(Must(Add(Must(Add(h0, h1)), l.bias_i))))

  var h2, h3, forgetGate *Node
  h2 = Must(Mul(l.wfx, inputVector))
  h3 = Must(Mul(l.wfh, prevHidden))
  forgetGate = Must(Sigmoid(Must(Add(Must(Add(h2, h3)), l.bias_f))))

  var h4, h5, outputGate *Node
  h4 = Must(Mul(l.wox, inputVector))
  h5 = Must(Mul(l.woh, prevHidden))
  outputGate = Must(Sigmoid(Must(Add(Must(Add(h4, h5)), l.bias_o))))

  var h6, h7, cellWrite *Node
  h6 = Must(Mul(l.wcx, inputVector))
  h7 = Must(Mul(l.wch, prevHidden))
  cellWrite = Must(Tanh(Must(Add(Must(Add(h6, h7)), l.bias_c))))

  // cell activations
  var retain, write *Node
  retain = Must(HadamardProd(forgetGate, prevCell))
  write = Must(HadamardProd(inputGate, cellWrite))
  cell := Must(Add(retain, write))
  hidden := Must(HadamardProd(outputGate, Must(Tanh(cell))))
  out = lstmout{
    hidden: hidden,
```

```
    cell: cell,
  }
  return
}

type lstmout struct {
  hidden, cell *Node
}
```

As we mentioned earlier, we will be including the code for a GRU-RNN too. This code is modular, so you will be able to swap out your LSTM for a GRU, extending the kinds of experiments you can do and the range of use cases you can address.

Let's create a file named gru.go. It will follow the same structure as lstm.go, but will have a reduced number of gates:

```
package main

import (
  "fmt"

  . "gorgonia.org/gorgonia"
  "gorgonia.org/tensor"
)

var Float = tensor.Float32

type contextualError interface {
  error
  Node() *Node
  Value() Value
  InstructionID() int
  Err() error
}

type GRU struct {

  // weights for mem
  u *Node
  w *Node
  b *Node

  // update gate
  uz *Node
  wz *Node
  bz *Node

  // reset gate
```

```
  ur  *Node
  wr  *Node
  br  *Node
  one *Node

  Name string // optional name
}

func MakeGRU(name string, g *ExprGraph, inputSize, hiddenSize int, dt
tensor.Dtype) GRU {
  // standard weights
  u := NewMatrix(g, dt, WithShape(hiddenSize, hiddenSize),
WithName(fmt.Sprintf("%v.u", name)), WithInit(GlorotN(1.0)))
  w := NewMatrix(g, dt, WithShape(hiddenSize, inputSize),
WithName(fmt.Sprintf("%v.w", name)), WithInit(GlorotN(1.0)))
  b := NewVector(g, dt, WithShape(hiddenSize), WithName(fmt.Sprintf("%v.b",
name)), WithInit(Zeroes()))

  // update gate
  uz := NewMatrix(g, dt, WithShape(hiddenSize, hiddenSize),
WithName(fmt.Sprintf("%v.uz", name)), WithInit(GlorotN(1.0)))
  wz := NewMatrix(g, dt, WithShape(hiddenSize, inputSize),
WithName(fmt.Sprintf("%v.wz", name)), WithInit(GlorotN(1.0)))
  bz := NewVector(g, dt, WithShape(hiddenSize),
WithName(fmt.Sprintf("%v.b_uz", name)), WithInit(Zeroes()))

  // reset gate
  ur := NewMatrix(g, dt, WithShape(hiddenSize, hiddenSize),
WithName(fmt.Sprintf("%v.ur", name)), WithInit(GlorotN(1.0)))
  wr := NewMatrix(g, dt, WithShape(hiddenSize, inputSize),
WithName(fmt.Sprintf("%v.wr", name)), WithInit(GlorotN(1.0)))
  br := NewVector(g, dt, WithShape(hiddenSize),
WithName(fmt.Sprintf("%v.bz", name)), WithInit(Zeroes()))

  ones := tensor.Ones(dt, hiddenSize)
  one := g.Constant(ones)
  gru := GRU{
    u: u,
    w: w,
    b: b,

    uz: uz,
    wz: wz,
    bz: bz,

    ur: ur,
    wr: wr,
    br: br,
```

```
      one: one,
    }
    return gru
}

func (l *GRU) Activate(x, prev *Node) (retVal *Node, err error) {
  // update gate
  uzh := Must(Mul(l.uz, prev))
  wzx := Must(Mul(l.wz, x))
  z := Must(Sigmoid(
    Must(Add(
      Must(Add(uzh, wzx)),
      l.bz))))

  // reset gate
  urh := Must(Mul(l.ur, prev))
  wrx := Must(Mul(l.wr, x))
  r := Must(Sigmoid(
    Must(Add(
      Must(Add(urh, wrx)),
      l.br))))

  // memory for hidden
  hiddenFilter := Must(Mul(l.u, Must(HadamardProd(r, prev))))
  wx := Must(Mul(l.w, x))
  mem := Must(Tanh(
    Must(Add(
      Must(Add(hiddenFilter, wx)),
      l.b))))

  omz := Must(Sub(l.one, z))
  omzh := Must(HadamardProd(omz, prev))
  upd := Must(HadamardProd(z, mem))
  retVal = Must(Add(upd, omzh))
  return
}

func (l *GRU) learnables() Nodes {
  retVal := make(Nodes, 0, 9)
  retVal = append(retVal, l.u, l.w, l.b, l.uz, l.wz, l.bz, l.ur, l.wr,
l.br)
  return retVal
}
```

As we continue to pull the pieces of our network together, we need a final layer of abstraction on top of our LSTM/GRU code—that of the network itself. The naming convention we are following is that of a *sequence-to-sequence* (or s2s) network. In our example, we are predicting the next character of text. This sequence is arbitrary, and can be words or sentences, or even a mapping between languages. Hence, we will be creating a s2s.go file.

Since this is effectively a larger neural network for containing the mini neural networks we defined in lstm.go/gru.go previously, the structure is similar. We can see that the LSTM is handling the input to our network (instead of the vanilla RNN cell), and that we have dummy nodes for handling inputs at t-0, as well as output nodes:

```go
package main

import (
    "encoding/json"
    "io"
    "log"
    "os"

    "github.com/pkg/errors"
    . "gorgonia.org/gorgonia"
    "gorgonia.org/tensor"
)

type seq2seq struct {
    in          LSTM
    dummyPrev *Node // vector
    dummyCell *Node // vector
    embedding *Node // NxM matrix, where M is the number of dimensions of the
embedding

    decoder *Node
    vocab []rune

    inVecs []*Node
    losses []*Node
    preds []*Node
    predvals []Value
    g *ExprGraph
    vm VM
}

// NewS2S creates a new Seq2Seq network. Input size is the size of the
embedding. Hidden size is the size of the hidden layer
func NewS2S(hiddenSize, embSize int, vocab []rune) *seq2seq {
```

```
g := NewGraph()
// in := MakeGRU("In", g, embSize, hiddenSize, Float)s
in := MakeLSTM(g, hiddenSize, embSize)
log.Printf("%q", vocab)

dummyPrev := NewVector(g, Float, WithShape(embSize), WithName("Dummy
Prev"), WithInit(Zeroes()))
dummyCell := NewVector(g, Float, WithShape(hiddenSize), WithName("Dummy
Cell"), WithInit(Zeroes()))
embedding := NewMatrix(g, Float, WithShape(len(vocab), embSize),
WithInit(GlorotN(1.0)), WithName("Embedding"))
decoder := NewMatrix(g, Float, WithShape(len(vocab), hiddenSize),
WithInit(GlorotN(1.0)), WithName("Output Decoder"))

    return &seq2seq{
      in: in,
      dummyPrev: dummyPrev,
      dummyCell: dummyCell,
      embedding: embedding,
      vocab: vocab,
      decoder: decoder,
      g: g,
    }
}

func (s *seq2seq) learnables() Nodes {
  retVal := make(Nodes, 0)
  retVal = append(retVal, s.in.learnables()...)
  retVal = append(retVal, s.embedding)
  retVal = append(retVal, s.decoder)
  return retVal
}
```

Since we're using a static graph, Gorgonia's `TapeMachine`, we will need a function to build our network when it is initialized. A number of these values will be replaced at runtime:

```
func (s *seq2seq) build() (cost *Node, err error) {
  // var prev *Node = s.dummyPrev
  prev := lstmout{
    hidden: s.dummyCell,
    cell: s.dummyCell,
  }
  s.predvals = make([]Value, maxsent)

  var prediction *Node
  for i := 0; i < maxsent; i++ {
    var vec *Node
    if i == 0 {
```

```
    vec = Must(Slice(s.embedding, S(0))) // dummy, to be replaced at
runtime
    } else {
      vec = Must(Mul(prediction, s.embedding))
    }
    s.inVecs = append(s.inVecs, vec)
    if prev, err = s.in.Activate(vec, prev); err != nil {
      return
    }
    prediction = Must(SoftMax(Must(Mul(s.decoder, prev.hidden))))
    s.preds = append(s.preds, prediction)
    Read(prediction, &s.predvals[i])

    logprob := Must(Neg(Must(Log(prediction))))
    loss := Must(Slice(logprob, S(0))) // dummy, to be replaced at runtime
    s.losses = append(s.losses, loss)

    if cost == nil {
      cost = loss
    } else {
      cost = Must(Add(cost, loss))
    }
  }

  _, err = Grad(cost, s.learnables()...)
  return
}
```

We can now define the training loop of the network itself:

```
func (s *seq2seq) train(in []rune) (err error) {

  for i := 0; i < maxsent; i++ {
    var currentRune, correctPrediction rune
    switch {
    case i == 0:
      currentRune = START
      correctPrediction = in[i]
    case i-1 == len(in)-1:
      currentRune = in[i-1]
      correctPrediction = END
    case i-1 >= len(in):
      currentRune = BLANK
      correctPrediction = BLANK
    default:
      currentRune = in[i-1]
      correctPrediction = in[i]
    }
```

```
    targetID := vocabIndex[correctPrediction]
    if i == 0 || i-1 >= len(in) {
      srcID := vocabIndex[currentRune]
      UnsafeLet(s.inVecs[i], S(srcID))
    }
    UnsafeLet(s.losses[i], S(targetID))

  }
  if s.vm == nil {
    s.vm = NewTapeMachine(s.g, BindDualValues())
  }
  s.vm.Reset()
  err = s.vm.RunAll()

  return
}
```

We also need a `predict` function so that after our model has been trained, we can sample it:

```
func (s *seq2seq) predict(in []rune) (output []rune, err error) {
  g2 := s.g.SubgraphRoots(s.preds...)
  vm := NewTapeMachine(g2)
  if err = vm.RunAll(); err != nil {
    return
  }
  defer vm.Close()
  for _, pred := range s.predvals {
    log.Printf("%v", pred.Shape())
    id := sample(pred)
    if id >= len(vocab) {
      log.Printf("Predicted %d. Len(vocab) %v", id, len(vocab))
      continue
    }
    r := vocab[id]

    output = append(output, r)
  }
  return
}
```

Training on a large text corpus can take a long time, so it will be useful to have a means of checkpointing our model so that we can save/load it from an arbitrary point in the training cycle:

```
func (s *seq2seq) checkpoint() (err error) {
  learnables := s.learnables()
  var f io.WriteCloser
```

```go
	if f, err = os.OpenFile("CHECKPOINT.bin",
os.O_CREATE|os.O_TRUNC|os.O_WRONLY, 0644); err != nil {
		return
	}
	defer f.Close()
	enc := json.NewEncoder(f)
	for _, l := range learnables {
		t := l.Value().(*tensor.Dense).Data() // []float32
		if err = enc.Encode(t); err != nil {
			return
		}
	}

	return nil
}

func (s *seq2seq) load() (err error) {
	learnables := s.learnables()
	var f io.ReadCloser
	if f, err = os.OpenFile("CHECKPOINT.bin", os.O_RDONLY, 0644); err != nil
{
		return
	}
	defer f.Close()
	dec := json.NewDecoder(f)
	for _, l := range learnables {
		t := l.Value().(*tensor.Dense).Data().([]float32)
		var data []float32
		if err = dec.Decode(&data); err != nil {
			return
		}
		if len(data) != len(t) {
			return errors.Errorf("Unserialized length %d. Expected length %d",
len(data), len(t))
		}
		copy(t, data)
	}
	return nil
}
```

Finally, we can define the meta-training loop. This is the loop that takes the s2s network, a solver, our data, and various hyperparameters:

```go
func train(s *seq2seq, epochs int, solver Solver, data []string) (err
error) {
	cost, err := s.build()
	if err != nil {
		return err
```

```
    }
    var costVal Value
    Read(cost, &costVal)

    model := NodesToValueGrads(s.learnables())
    for e := 0; e < epochs; e++ {
      shuffle(data)

      for _, sentence := range data {
        asRunes := []rune(sentence)
        if err = s.train(asRunes); err != nil {
          return
        }
        if err = solver.Step(model); err != nil {
          return
        }
      }
      // if e%100 == 0 {
      log.Printf("Cost for epoch %d: %1.10f\n", e, costVal)
      // }

    }

    return nil

}
```

Before we build and execute our network, we will add a small visualization tool that will assist in any troubleshooting we need to do. Visualization is a powerful tool when working with data generally, and in our case, it allows us to peek inside our neural network so that we can understand what it is doing. Specifically, we will generate heatmaps that we can use to track changes in our network's weights throughout the training process. This way, we can ensure that they are changing (that is, that our network is learning).

Create a file called heatmap.go:

```
package main

import (
    "image/color"
    "math"

    "github.com/pkg/errors"
    "gonum.org/v1/gonum/mat"
    "gonum.org/v1/plot"
    "gonum.org/v1/plot/palette/moreland"
    "gonum.org/v1/plot/plotter"
```

```
    "gonum.org/v1/plot/vg"
    "gorgonia.org/tensor"
)

type heatmap struct {
    x mat.Matrix
}

func (m heatmap) Dims() (c, r int) { r, c = m.x.Dims(); return c, r }
func (m heatmap) Z(c, r int) float64 { return m.x.At(r, c) }
func (m heatmap) X(c int) float64 { return float64(c) }
func (m heatmap) Y(r int) float64 { return float64(r) }

type ticks []string

func (t ticks) Ticks(min, max float64) []plot.Tick {
    var retVal []plot.Tick
    for i := math.Trunc(min); i <= max; i++ {
        retVal = append(retVal, plot.Tick{Value: i, Label: t[int(i)]})
    }
    return retVal
}

func Heatmap(a *tensor.Dense) (p *plot.Plot, H, W vg.Length, err error) {
    switch a.Dims() {
    case 1:
        original := a.Shape()
        a.Reshape(original[0], 1)
        defer a.Reshape(original...)
    case 2:
    default:
        return nil, 0, 0, errors.Errorf("Can't do a tensor with shape %v",
a.Shape())
    }

    m, err := tensor.ToMat64(a, tensor.UseUnsafe())
    if err != nil {
        return nil, 0, 0, err
    }

    pal := moreland.ExtendedBlackBody().Palette(256)
    // lum, _ := moreland.NewLuminance([]color.Color{color.Gray{0},
color.Gray{255}})
    // pal := lum.Palette(256)

    hm := plotter.NewHeatMap(heatmap{m}, pal)
    if p, err = plot.New(); err != nil {
        return nil, 0, 0, err
```

```
    }
    hm.NaN = color.RGBA{0, 0, 0, 0} // black
    p.Add(hm)

    sh := a.Shape()
    H = vg.Length(sh[0])*vg.Centimeter + vg.Centimeter
    W = vg.Length(sh[1])*vg.Centimeter + vg.Centimeter
    return p, H, W, nil
}

func Avg(a []float64) (retVal float64) {
    for _, v := range a {
        retVal += v
    }

    return retVal / float64(len(a))
}
```

We can now pull all the pieces together and create our `main.go` file. Here, we will set our hyperparameters, parse our input, and kick off our main training loop:

```
package main

import (
  "flag"
  "fmt"
  "io/ioutil"
  "log"
  "os"
  "runtime/pprof"

  . "gorgonia.org/gorgonia"
  "gorgonia.org/tensor"
)

var cpuprofile = flag.String("cpuprofile", "", "write cpu profile to file")
var memprofile = flag.String("memprofile", "", "write memory profile to
this file")

const (
  embeddingSize = 20
  maxOut = 30

  // gradient update stuff
  l2reg = 0.000001
  learnrate = 0.01
  clipVal = 5.0
)
```

```go
var trainiter = flag.Int("iter", 5, "How many iterations to train")

// various global variable inits
var epochSize = -1
var inputSize = -1
var outputSize = -1

var corpus string

func init() {
  buf, err := ioutil.ReadFile("shakespeare.txt")
  if err != nil {
    panic(err)
  }
  corpus = string(buf)
}

var dt tensor.Dtype = tensor.Float32

func main() {
  flag.Parse()
  if *cpuprofile != "" {
    f, err := os.Create(*cpuprofile)
    if err != nil {
      log.Fatal(err)
    }
    pprof.StartCPUProfile(f)
    defer pprof.StopCPUProfile()
  }

  hiddenSize := 100

  s2s := NewS2S(hiddenSize, embeddingSize, vocab)
  solver := NewRMSPropSolver(WithLearnRate(learnrate), WithL2Reg(l2reg),
WithClip(clipVal), WithBatchSize(float64(len(sentences))))
  for k, v := range vocabIndex {
    log.Printf("%q %v", k, v)
  }

  // p, h, w, err := Heatmap(s2s.decoder.Value().(*tensor.Dense))
  // p.Save(w, h, "embn0.png")

  if err := train(s2s, 300, solver, sentences); err != nil {
    panic(err)
  }
  out, err := s2s.predict([]rune(corpus))
  if err != nil {
    panic(err)
```

```
    }
    fmt.Printf("OUT %q\n", out)

    p, h, w, err = Heatmap(s2s.decoder.Value().(*tensor.Dense))
    p.Save(w, h, "embn.png")
}
```

Now, let's run `go run *.go` and observe the output:

```
2019/05/25 23:52:03 Cost for epoch 31: 250.7806701660
2019/05/25 23:52:19 Cost for epoch 32: 176.0116729736
2019/05/25 23:52:35 Cost for epoch 33: 195.0501556396
2019/05/25 23:52:50 Cost for epoch 34: 190.6829681396
2019/05/25 23:53:06 Cost for epoch 35: 181.1398162842
```

We can see that early in our network's life, the cost, which measures the degree to which our network is optimized, is high and fluctuating.

After the designated number of epochs, an output prediction will be made:

```
OUT ['S' 'a' 'K' 'a' 'g' 'y' 'h' ',' '\x04' 'a' 'g' 'a' 't' '\x04' '\x04' '
' 's' 'h' 'h' 'h' 'h' 'h' ' ' ' ' ' ' ' ' ' ' ' ' ' ' ' ' ' ' ' ' ' ' ' ' ']
```

You can now experiment with hyperparameters and tweaks, such as using GRU instead of LSTM units, and explore bias initialization in an effort to optimize your network further and produce better predictions.

Summary

In this chapter, we have covered what an RNN is and how to train one. We have seen that, in order to effectively model long-term dependencies and overcome training challenges, changes to a standard RNN are necessary, including additional information-across-time control mechanisms that are provided by GRU/LSTM units. We built such a network in Gorgonia.

In next chapter, we will learn how to build a CNN and how to tune some of the hyperparameters.

Further reading

- *Training Recurrent Neural Networks, Ilya Sutskever,* available at `http://www.cs.utoronto.ca/~ilya/pubs/ilya_sutskever_phd_thesis.pdf`
- *Long Short-Term Memory, Hochreiter, Sepp,* and *Jurgen Schmidhuber,* available at `https://www.researchgate.net/publication/13853244_Long_Short-term_Memory`
- *Empirical Evaluation of Gated Recurrent Neural Networks on Sequence Modeling, Bengio et al,* available at `https://arxiv.org/abs/1412.3555`

6
Object Recognition with Convolutional Neural Networks

Now it's time to get to some computer vision or image classification problems that are a little more general than our earlier MNIST handwriting example. A lot of the same principles apply, but we will be using some new types of operations to build **Convolutional Neural Networks (CNNs)**.

This chapter will cover the following topics:

- Introduction to CNNs
- Building an example CNN
- Assessing the results and making improvements

Introduction to CNNs

CNNs are a class of deep neural networks—they are well suited to data with several channels and are sensitive to the locality of the information contained within the inputs fed into the network. This makes CNNs well suited for tasks associated with computer vision such as facial recognition, image classification, scene labeling, and more.

What is a CNN?

CNNs, also known as **ConvNets**, are a class or a category of neural networks that are generally accepted to be very good at image classification, that is to say, they are very good at distinguishing cats from dogs, cars from planes, and many other common classification tasks.

A CNN typically consists of convolution layers, activation layers, and pooling layers. However, it has been structured specifically to take advantage of the fact that the inputs are typically images, and take advantage of the fact that some parts of the image are very likely to be next to each other.

They are actually fairly similar implementation wise to the feedforward networks that we have covered in earlier chapters.

Normal feedforward versus ConvNet

In general, a neural network receives a single vector as input (such as our MNIST example in `Chapter 3`, *Beyond Basic Neural Networks – Autoencoders and RBMs*) and then goes through several hidden layers, before arriving at the end with our inference for the result. This is fine for images that aren't that big; when our images become larger, however, as they usually are in most real-life applications, we want to ensure that we aren't building immensely large hidden layers to process them correctly.

Of course, one of the convenient features that is present in our ideas with tensors is the fact that we don't actually have to feed a vector into the model; we can feed something a little more complicated and with more dimensions. Basically, what we want to do with a CNN is that we want to have neurons arranged in three dimensions: height, width, and depth—what we mean by depth here is the number of colors in our color system, in our case being red, green, and blue.

Instead of trying to connect every neuron in a layer together, we will try to reduce it so that it is more manageable and less likely to be overfitted for our sample size, as we won't be trying to train every single pixel of the input.

Layers

Of course, CNNs use layers, and we will need to talk about some of these layers in more detail, because we haven't discussed them yet; in general, there are three main layers in a CNN: convolutional layers, pooling layers, and fully connected layers (these are the ones you've already seen).

Convolutional layer

Convolutional layers are part of the name of this neural network and form a very important part of the neural network architecture. It can be broadly explained as scanning across the image to find certain features. We create a small filter, which we then slide across the entire image according to our desired stride.

So, for example, the first cell of the output would be calculated by finding the **Dot Product** of our 3 x 3 filter with the top-left corner of our **Image**, as shown in the following diagram:

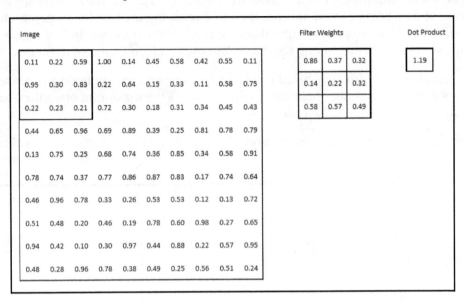

And if your stride was one, it would shift one column right and continue, as shown here:

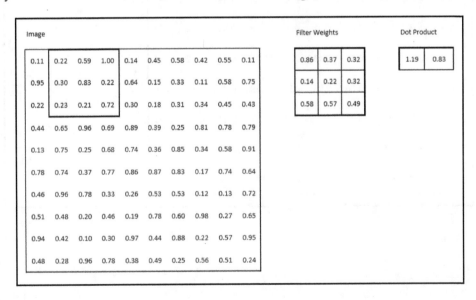

This would then continue until we had our entire output.

Pooling layer

Pooling layers are commonly put in between convolutional layers; they are meant to reduce the volume of data being passed around, therefore reducing the number of parameters, as well as reducing the amount of computation required by the network. In this case, we are *pooling* numbers together by taking the maximum over a given region of numbers.

These layers also work similarly to the convolutional layers; they apply on a predetermined grid and perform the pooling operation. In this case, it is the maximum operation, so it will take the highest value within the grid.

For example, in a max pooling operation on a 2 x 2 grid, the first cell of output will come from the top left, as follows:

Input										MaxPool
0.96	0.28	0.80	0.14	0.10	0.86	0.64	0.11	0.73	0.28	0.96
0.92	0.20	0.29	0.53	0.45	0.33	0.54	0.11	0.34	0.59	
0.97	0.64	0.34	0.53	0.74	0.20	0.47	0.52	0.42	0.53	
0.50	0.52	0.65	0.72	0.98	0.11	0.44	0.44	0.10	0.43	
0.69	0.96	0.40	0.56	0.91	0.95	0.98	0.34	0.82	0.82	
0.22	0.95	0.35	0.13	0.43	0.93	0.16	0.37	0.62	0.14	
0.81	0.74	0.46	0.86	0.56	0.57	0.29	0.20	0.45	0.65	
0.68	0.90	0.97	0.94	0.61	0.96	0.52	0.61	0.73	0.23	
0.97	0.91	0.88	0.22	0.46	0.56	0.40	0.12	0.75	0.87	
0.52	0.64	0.96	0.35	0.63	0.35	0.22	0.42	0.93	0.43	

And with a stride of two, the second will come from the grid shifted right two rows, as shown here:

Input												MaxPool	
0.96	0.28	0.80	0.14	0.10	0.86	0.64	0.11	0.73	0.28			0.96	0.80
0.92	0.20	0.29	0.53	0.45	0.33	0.54	0.11	0.34	0.59				
0.97	0.64	0.34	0.53	0.74	0.20	0.47	0.52	0.42	0.53				
0.50	0.52	0.65	0.72	0.98	0.11	0.44	0.44	0.10	0.43				
0.69	0.96	0.40	0.56	0.91	0.95	0.98	0.34	0.82	0.82				
0.22	0.95	0.35	0.13	0.43	0.93	0.16	0.37	0.62	0.14				
0.81	0.74	0.46	0.86	0.56	0.57	0.29	0.20	0.45	0.65				
0.68	0.90	0.97	0.94	0.61	0.96	0.52	0.61	0.73	0.23				
0.97	0.91	0.88	0.22	0.46	0.56	0.40	0.12	0.75	0.87				
0.52	0.64	0.96	0.35	0.63	0.35	0.22	0.42	0.93	0.43				

Basic structure

Now that you understand the layers, let's talk about the basic structure of a CNN. A CNN consists broadly of the following: an input layer, and then several layers of convolutional layers, activation layers, and pooling layers, before ending in a fully connected layer at the end to get to our final results.

The basic structure looks a little like the following:

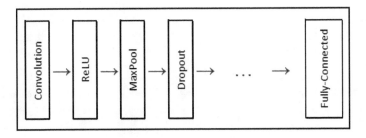

Building an example CNN

To illustrate how a CNN works in practice, we will be building a model to recognize whether an object in a photo is a cat or not. The dataset we are using has more depth than this, but it would take a rather long time to train it to correctly classify everything. It is fairly trivial to extend the example to classify everything, but we would rather not be sitting there for a week waiting for the model to train.

For our example, we will be using the following structure:

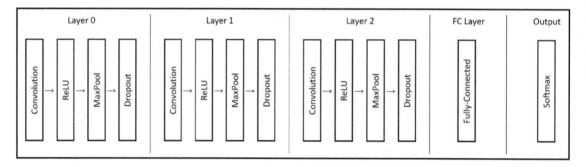

CIFAR-10

We are using CIFAR-10 for our example this time instead of MNIST. As such, we do not have the convenience of using the already convenient MNIST loader. Let's quickly go through what it takes to load this new dataset!

We will be using the binary format for CIFAR-10, which you can download here: https://www.cs.toronto.edu/~kriz/cifar.html.

This dataset was put together by Alex Krizhevsky, Vinod Nair, and Geoffrey Hinton. It consists of 60,000 tiny images 32 pixels high by 32 pixels wide. The binary format of CIFAR-10 is laid out as follows:

```
<1 x label><3072 x pixel>
<1 x label><3072 x pixel>
<1 x label><3072 x pixel>
<1 x label><3072 x pixel>
<1 x label><3072 x pixel>
<1 x label><3072 x pixel>
...
<1 x label><3072 x pixel>
```

It should be noted that it is not delimited or does not have any other information for validation of the file; as such, you should ensure that the MD5 checksum for the file that you have downloaded matches that on the website. As the structure is relatively simple, we can just pull the binary file straight into Go and parse it accordingly.

The 3,072 pixels are actually three layers of red, green, and blue values from 0 to 255, over a 32 x 32 grid in row-major order, so this gives us our image data.

The label is a number from **0** to **9**, representing one of the following categories respectively:

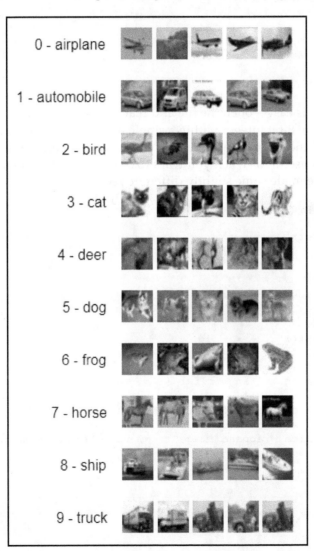

CIFAR-10 comes in six files, five training set files of 10,000 images each and one test set file of 10,000 images:

```
case "train":
    arrayFiles = []string{
        "data_batch_1.bin",
        "data_batch_2.bin",
        "data_batch_3.bin",
        "data_batch_4.bin",
        "data_batch_5.bin",
    }
case "test":
    arrayFiles = []string{
        "test_batch.bin",
    }
}
```

Importing this in Go is easy—open the file and read the raw bytes. As every single underlying value is an 8-bit integer within a single byte, we can just cast it to whatever we want. If you wanted the single integer values, you could just convert them all into unsigned 8-bit integers; this is useful for when you want to convert the data into an image. You'll find, however, we've made some slightly different decisions in the code, as follows:

```
f, err := os.Open(filepath.Join(loc, targetFile))
if err != nil {
    log.Fatal(err)
}

defer f.Close()
cifar, err := ioutil.ReadAll(f)

if err != nil {
    log.Fatal(err)
}

for index, element := range cifar {
    if index%3073 == 0 {
        labelSlice = append(labelSlice, float64(element))
    } else {
        imageSlice = append(imageSlice, pixelWeight(element))
    }
}
```

As we are interested in using this data for our deep learning algorithm, it is prudent to not stray too far from our happy medium between 0 and 1. We're reusing pixel weight from the MNIST example, as shown here:

```
func pixelWeight(px byte) float64 {
    retVal := float64(px)/pixelRange*0.9 + 0.1
    if retVal == 1.0 {
        return 0.999
    }
    return retVal
}
```

This will convert all our pixel values from 0 to 255 to a range between 0.1 and 1.0.

Similarly, for our labels, we will be using one-hot encoding again, encoding the desired label at 0.9 and everything else at 0.1, as shown in the following code:

```
labelBacking := make([]float64, len(labelSlice)*numLabels,
len(labelSlice)*numLabels)
labelBacking = labelBacking[:0]
for i := 0; i < len(labelSlice); i++ {
    for j := 0; j < numLabels; j++ {
        if j == int(labelSlice[i]) {
            labelBacking = append(labelBacking, 0.9)
        } else {
            labelBacking = append(labelBacking, 0.1)
        }
    }
}
```

We've packaged this into a convenient Load function so we can call it from our code. It'll return two conveniently shaped tensors for us to work with. This gives us a function that can import both the train and test sets:

```
func Load(typ, loc string) (inputs, targets tensor.Tensor, err error) {

    ...

    inputs = tensor.New(tensor.WithShape(len(labelSlice), 3, 32, 32),
tensor.WithBacking(imageSlice))
    targets = tensor.New(tensor.WithShape(len(labelSlice), numLabels),
tensor.WithBacking(labelBacking))
    return
}
```

This allows us to load the data in my `main` by calling the following:

```
if inputs, targets, err = cifar.Load("train", loc); err != nil {
    log.Fatal(err)
}
```

Epochs and batch size

We'll choose `10` epochs for this example so that the code can be trained in less than an hour. It should be noted that 10 epochs will only get us to around 20% accuracy, so do not be alarmed if you find the resulting model does not appear accurate; you will need to train it for much longer, maybe even around 1,000 epochs. On a modern computer, an epoch takes around three minutes to complete; for the sake of not requiring three days to complete this example, we've chosen to abbreviate the training process and will leave it as an exercise to assess the results of more epochs, as shown here:

```
var (
    epochs = flag.Int("epochs", 10, "Number of epochs to train for")
    dataset = flag.String("dataset", "train", "Which dataset to train on?
Valid options are \"train\" or \"test\"")
    dtype = flag.String("dtype", "float64", "Which dtype to use")
    batchsize = flag.Int("batchsize", 100, "Batch size")
    cpuprofile = flag.String("cpuprofile", "", "CPU profiling")
)
```

Note that this model will consume a fairly large amount of memory; a `batchsize` of `100` can still mean you will need around 4 GB of memory. If you don't have this amount available without resorting to swapping memory, you may want to lower the batch size to make the code perform better on your computer.

Accuracy

As this model takes much longer to converge, we should also add a rudimentary metric to track our accuracy. In order to do this, we must first extract our labels from the data - which we can do as below:

```
// get label
    yRowT, _ := yVal.Slice(sli{j, j + 1})
    yRow := yRowT.Data().([]float64)
    var rowLabel int
    var yRowHigh float64

    for k := 0; k < 10; k++ {
```

```
if k == 0 {
    rowLabel = 0
    yRowHigh = yRow[k]
} else if yRow[k] > yRowHigh {
    rowLabel = k
    yRowHigh = yRow[k]
}
}
```

We must then get our prediction from the output data:

```
yOutput2 := tensor.New(tensor.WithShape(bs, 10),
tensor.WithBacking(arrayOutput2))

// get prediction
    predRowT, _ := yOutput2.Slice(sli{j, j + 1})
    predRow := predRowT.Data().([]float64)
    var rowGuess int
    var predRowHigh float64

    // guess result
    for k := 0; k < 10; k++ {
        if k == 0 {
            rowGuess = 0
            predRowHigh = predRow[k]
        } else if predRow[k] > predRowHigh {
            rowGuess = k
            predRowHigh = predRow[k]
        }
    }
}
```

We can then use this to update our accuracy metric. The amount by which it is updated is scaled by the number of examples - so that our output will be a percentage figure.

```
if rowLabel == rowGuess {
    accuracyGuess += 1.0 / float64(numExamples)
}
```

This give us a broad *accuracy* metric that we can use to gauge our training progress.

Constructing the layers

We can think of our layer structure having four parts. We are going to have three convolutional layers and one fully connected layer. Our first two layers are extremely similar - they follow the convolution-ReLU-MaxPool-dropout structure that we've described previously:

```
// Layer 0
if c0, err = gorgonia.Conv2d(x, m.w0, tensor.Shape{5, 5}, []int{1, 1},
[]int{1, 1}, []int{1, 1}); err != nil {
    return errors.Wrap(err, "Layer 0 Convolution failed")
}
if a0, err = gorgonia.Rectify(c0); err != nil {
    return errors.Wrap(err, "Layer 0 activation failed")
}
if p0, err = gorgonia.MaxPool2D(a0, tensor.Shape{2, 2}, []int{0, 0},
[]int{2, 2}); err != nil {
    return errors.Wrap(err, "Layer 0 Maxpooling failed")
}
if l0, err = gorgonia.Dropout(p0, m.d0); err != nil {
    return errors.Wrap(err, "Unable to apply a dropout")
}
```

Our following layer is similar - we just need to join it to the output of our previous one:

```
// Layer 1
if c1, err = gorgonia.Conv2d(l0, m.w1, tensor.Shape{5, 5}, []int{1, 1},
[]int{1, 1}, []int{1, 1}); err != nil {
    return errors.Wrap(err, "Layer 1 Convolution failed")
}
if a1, err = gorgonia.Rectify(c1); err != nil {
    return errors.Wrap(err, "Layer 1 activation failed")
}
if p1, err = gorgonia.MaxPool2D(a1, tensor.Shape{2, 2}, []int{0, 0},
[]int{2, 2}); err != nil {
    return errors.Wrap(err, "Layer 1 Maxpooling failed")
}
if l1, err = gorgonia.Dropout(p1, m.d1); err != nil {
    return errors.Wrap(err, "Unable to apply a dropout to layer 1")
}
```

The following layer is essentially the same, but there is a slight change to prepare it for the change to the fully connected layer:

```
// Layer 2
if c2, err = gorgonia.Conv2d(l1, m.w2, tensor.Shape{5, 5}, []int{1, 1},
[]int{1, 1}, []int{1, 1}); err != nil {
    return errors.Wrap(err, "Layer 2 Convolution failed")
}
if a2, err = gorgonia.Rectify(c2); err != nil {
    return errors.Wrap(err, "Layer 2 activation failed")
}
if p2, err = gorgonia.MaxPool2D(a2, tensor.Shape{2, 2}, []int{0, 0},
[]int{2, 2}); err != nil {
    return errors.Wrap(err, "Layer 2 Maxpooling failed")
}

var r2 *gorgonia.Node
b, c, h, w := p2.Shape()[0], p2.Shape()[1], p2.Shape()[2], p2.Shape()[3]
if r2, err = gorgonia.Reshape(p2, tensor.Shape{b, c * h * w}); err != nil {
    return errors.Wrap(err, "Unable to reshape layer 2")
}
if l2, err = gorgonia.Dropout(r2, m.d2); err != nil {
    return errors.Wrap(err, "Unable to apply a dropout on layer 2")
}
```

Layer 3 is something we're already very familiar with—the fully connected layer—here, we have a fairly simple structure. We can certainly add more tiers to this layer (and this has been done by many different architectures before as well, with differing levels of success). This layer is demonstrated in the following code:

```
// Layer 3
log.Printf("l2 shape %v", l2.Shape())
log.Printf("w3 shape %v", m.w3.Shape())
if fc, err = gorgonia.Mul(l2, m.w3); err != nil {
    return errors.Wrapf(err, "Unable to multiply l2 and w3")
}
if a3, err = gorgonia.Rectify(fc); err != nil {
    return errors.Wrapf(err, "Unable to activate fc")
}
if l3, err = gorgonia.Dropout(a3, m.d3); err != nil {
    return errors.Wrapf(err, "Unable to apply a dropout on layer 3")
}
```

Loss function and solver

We will be using the ordinary cross-entropy loss function here, which can be implemented as follows:

```
losses :=
gorgonia.Must(gorgonia.HadamardProd(gorgonia.Must(gorgonia.Log(m.out)), y))
cost := gorgonia.Must(gorgonia.Sum(losses))
cost = gorgonia.Must(gorgonia.Neg(cost))

if _, err = gorgonia.Grad(cost, m.learnables()...); err != nil {
    log.Fatal(err)
}
```

Together with that, we will be using the Gorgonia tape machine and the RMSprop solver, as shown here:

```
vm := gorgonia.NewTapeMachine(g, gorgonia.WithPrecompiled(prog, locMap),
gorgonia.BindDualValues(m.learnables()...))
solver := gorgonia.NewRMSPropSolver(gorgonia.WithBatchSize(float64(bs)))
```

Test set output

At the end of our training, we should pit our model against the test set.

First, we should import our test data as follows:

```
if inputs, targets, err = cifar.Load("test", loc); err != nil {
    log.Fatal(err)
}
```

Then, we need recalculate our batches as the test set is sized differently from the train set:

```
batches = inputs.Shape()[0] / bs
bar = pb.New(batches)
bar.SetRefreshRate(time.Second)
bar.SetMaxWidth(80)
```

We then need to just add a quick way to track our results and output our results for later inspection by inserting the following code into the accuracy metric calculation code described earlier in the chapter:

```
// slices to store our output
var testActual, testPred []int

// store our output into the slices within the loop
testActual = append(testActual, rowLabel)
testPred = append(testPred, rowGuess)
```

And finally, at the end of our run through the entire test set - write the data out to text files:

```
printIntSlice("testActual.txt", testActual)
printIntSlice("testPred.txt", testPred)
```

Let's now assess the results.

Assessing the results

As mentioned previously, the example trained over 10 epochs is not particularly accurate. You will need to train it over many epochs to get better results. If you have been watching the cost and accuracy of the model, you'll find that cost will stay relatively flat as accuracy increased over the number of epochs, as shown in the following graph:

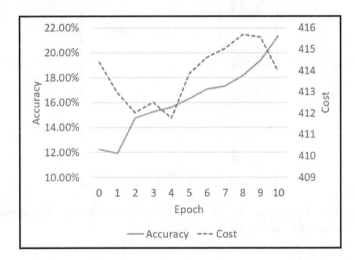

It is still useful to explore the results to see how the model is performing; we'll specifically look at cats:

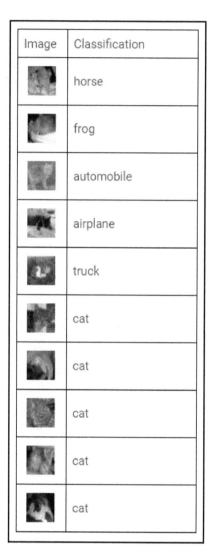

Image	Classification
	horse
	frog
	automobile
	airplane
	truck
	cat
	cat
	cat
	cat
	cat

As we can see, it currently appears to do much better with cats in very specific positions. Obviously, we need to find a solution to train it faster.

GPU acceleration

Convolution and its associated operations tend to do very well on GPU acceleration. You saw earlier that our GPU acceleration had minimal impact, but it is extremely useful for building CNNs. All we need to do is add the magical `'cuda'` build tag, as shown here:

```
go build -tags='cuda'
```

As we tend to be more memory constrained on GPUs, be aware that the same batch size may not work on your GPU. The model as mentioned previously uses around 4 GB of memory, so you will probably want to reduce the batch size if you have less than 6 GB of GPU memory (because presumably, you will be using about 1 GB for your normal desktop). If your model is running very slowly, or the CUDA version of your executable just fails, it would be prudent to check if being out of memory is the issue. You can do this using the NVIDIA SMI utility and getting it to check your memory every second, as shown here:

```
nvidia-smi -l 1
```

This will tend to produce the following report every second; watching it while your code runs will tell you broadly how much GPU memory your code is consuming:

```
+-----------------------------------------------------------------------------+
| NVIDIA-SMI 417.35       Driver Version: 417.35       CUDA Version: 10.0      |
|-------------------------------+----------------------+----------------------+
| GPU  Name            TCC/WDDM | Bus-Id        Disp.A | Volatile Uncorr. ECC |
| Fan  Temp  Perf  Pwr:Usage/Cap|         Memory-Usage | GPU-Util  Compute M. |
|===============================+======================+======================|
|   0  GeForce GTX 1080    WDDM | 00000000:01:00.0  On |                  N/A |
| 18%   49C    P8    14W / 200W |    788MiB /  8192MiB |      0%      Default |
+-------------------------------+----------------------+----------------------+

+-----------------------------------------------------------------------------+
| Processes:                                                       GPU Memory |
|  GPU       PID   Type   Process name                             Usage      |
|=============================================================================|
|    0      1144   C+G    Insufficient Permissions                 N/A        |
|    0      5040   C+G    ...6)\Google\Chrome\Application\chrome.exe N/A       |
|    0      7832   C+G    C:\Windows\explorer.exe                   N/A        |
|    0      8576   C+G    ...t_cw5n1h2txyewy\ShellExperienceHost.exe N/A      |
|    0      9080   C+G    ...dows.Cortana_cw5n1h2txyewy\SearchUI.exe N/A      |
|    0     14448   C+G    ...mmersiveControlPanel\SystemSettings.exe N/A      |
|    0     14544   C+G    ...2.0_x64__8wekyb3d8bbwe\WinStore.App.exe N/A      |
|    0     16132   C+G    ...sktop App\AcWebBrowser\acwebbrowser.exe N/A      |
|    0     18252   C+G    ...cal\mattermost\app-4.1.2\Mattermost.exe N/A      |
|    0     56948   C+G    ...rogram Files\Microsoft VS Code\Code.exe N/A      |
+-----------------------------------------------------------------------------+
```

Let's quickly compare the performance between CPU and GPU versions of our code. The CPU version takes broadly around three minutes per epoch, as shown in the following code:

```
2018/12/30 13:23:36 Batches 500
2018/12/30 13:26:23 Epoch 0 |
2018/12/30 13:29:15 Epoch 1 |
2018/12/30 13:32:01 Epoch 2 |
2018/12/30 13:34:47 Epoch 3 |
2018/12/30 13:37:33 Epoch 4 |
2018/12/30 13:40:19 Epoch 5 |
2018/12/30 13:43:05 Epoch 6 |
2018/12/30 13:45:50 Epoch 7 |
2018/12/30 13:48:36 Epoch 8 |
2018/12/30 13:51:22 Epoch 9 |
2018/12/30 13:51:55 Epoch Test |
```

The GPU version takes around two minutes thirty seconds per epoch, as shown in the following code:

```
2018/12/30 12:57:56 Batches 500
2018/12/30 13:00:24 Epoch 0
2018/12/30 13:02:49 Epoch 1
2018/12/30 13:05:15 Epoch 2
2018/12/30 13:07:40 Epoch 3
2018/12/30 13:10:04 Epoch 4
2018/12/30 13:12:29 Epoch 5
2018/12/30 13:14:55 Epoch 6
2018/12/30 13:17:21 Epoch 7
2018/12/30 13:19:45 Epoch 8
2018/12/30 13:22:10 Epoch 9
2018/12/30 13:22:40 Epoch Test
```

A future version of Gorgonia will also include support for better operations; this is currently in testing, and you can use it by importing `gorgonia.org/gorgonia/ops/nn` and replacing your `Conv2d`, `Rectify`, `MaxPool2D`, and `Dropout` calls from their Gorgonia versions with their `nnops` version, An example of a slightly different `Layer 0` is as follows:

```
if c0, err = nnops.Conv2d(x, m.w0, tensor.Shape{3, 3}, []int{1, 1},
[]int{1, 1}, []int{1, 1}); err != nil {
    return errors.Wrap(err, "Layer 0 Convolution failed")
}
if a0, err = nnops.Rectify(c0); err != nil {
    return errors.Wrap(err, "Layer 0 activation failed")
}
if p0, err = nnops.MaxPool2D(a0, tensor.Shape{2, 2}, []int{0, 0}, []int{2,
2}); err != nil {
```

```
        return errors.Wrap(err, "Layer 0 Maxpooling failed")
    }
    if l0, err = nnops.Dropout(p0, m.d0); err != nil {
        return errors.Wrap(err, "Unable to apply a dropout")
    }
```

As an exercise, replace all the necessary operations and run it to see how it is different.

CNN weaknesses

CNNs actually have a fairly major weakness: they are not orientation invariant, which means that if you were to feed the same image in, but upside down, the network is likely to not recognize it at all. One of the ways we can ensure this is not the case is to train the model with different rotations; however, there are better architectures that can solve this problem, which we will discuss later in this book.

They are also not scale invariant. Feeding it the same image much smaller or much larger makes it likely to fail. If you think back to why this is the case, it's because we are building the model based on a filter of a very specific size on a very specific group of pixels.

You have also seen that the model is very slow to train in general, especially on the CPU. We can get around this somewhat by using the GPU instead, but overall, it is an expensive process and can take several days to complete.

Summary

You have now learned how to build a CNN and how to tune some of the hyperparameters (such as the number of epochs and batch sizes) in order to get the desired result and get it running smoothly on different computers.

As an exercise, you should try training this model to recognize MNIST digits, and even change around the structure of the convolutional layers; try Batch Normalization, and perhaps even more weights in the fully connected layer.

The next chapter will give an introduction to reinforcement learning and Q-learning and how to build a DQN and solve a maze.

Further reading

- *Character-Level Convolutional Networks for Text Classification* by *Xiang Zhang, Junbo Zhao* and *Yann LeCun*
- *U-Net: Convolutional Networks for Biomedical Image Segmentation* by *Olaf Ronneberger, Philipp Fischer,* and *Thomas Brox*
- *Faster R-CNN: Towards Real-Time Object Detection with Region Proposal Networks* by *Shaoqing Ren, Kaiming He, Ross Girshick,* and *Jian Sun*
- *Long-term Recurrent Convolutional Networks for Visual Recognition and Description* by *Jeff Donahue, Lisa Anne Hendricks, Marcus Rohrbach, Subhashini Venugopalan, Sergio Guadarrama, Kate Saenko,* and *Trevor Darrell*

Maze Solving with Deep Q-Networks

7

Imagine for a moment that your data is not a discrete body of text or a carefully cleaned set of records from your organization's data warehouse. Perhaps you would like to train an agent to navigate an environment. How would you begin to solve this problem? None of the techniques that we have covered so far are suitable for such a task. We need to think about how we can train our model in quite a different way to make this problem tractable. Additionally, with use cases where the problem can be framed as an agent exploring and attaining a reward from an environment, from game playing to personalized news recommendations, **Deep Q-Networks** (**DQNs**) are useful tools in our arsenal of deep learning techniques.

Reinforcement learning (**RL**) has been described by Yann LeCun (who was instrumental in the development of **Convolutional Neural Networks** (**CNNs**) and, at the time of writing, the director of Facebook AI Research) as the cherry on the cake of machine learning methods. In this analogy, unsupervised learning is the cake and supervised learning is the icing. What's important for us to understand here is that RL only solves a very specific case of problems, despite offering the promise of model-free learning, where you simply offer some scalar reward as your model optimizes successfully toward the goal you have specified.

This chapter will offer a brief background on why this is, and how RL fits into the picture more generally. Specifically, we will cover the following topics:

- What is a DQN?
- Learning about the Q-learning algorithm
- Learning about how to train a DQN
- Building a DQN for solving mazes

What is a DQN?

As you will learn, a DQN is not that different from the standard feedforward and convolutional networks that we have covered so far. Indeed, all the standard ingredients are present:

- A representation of our data (in this example, the state of our maze and the agent trying to navigate through it)
- Standard layers to process a representation of our maze, which also includes standard operations between these layers, such as the `Tanh` activation function
- An output layer with a linear activation, which gives you predictions

Here, our predictions represent possible moves affecting the state of our input. In the case of maze solving, we are trying to predict moves that produce the maximum (and cumulative) expected reward for our player, which ultimately leads to the maze's exit. These predictions occur as part of a training loop, where the learning algorithm uses a *Gamma* variable as a decaying-over-time variable that balances the exploration of the environment's state space and the exploitation of knowledge gleaned by building up a map of actions, states, or rewards.

Let's introduce a number of new concepts. First, we need an *m* x *n* matrix that represents the rewards, *R*, for a given *state* (that is, a row) and *action* (that is, a column). We also need a *Q* table. This is a matrix (initialized with zero values) that represents the memory of the agent (that is, our player trying to find its way through the maze), or a history of states, actions taken, and their rewards.

These two matrices relate to each other. We can determine the memory (*Q* table) of our agent with respect to the table of known rewards with the following formula:

$$Q(state, action) = R(state, action) + Gamma * Max[Q(next\ state, all\ actions)]$$

Here, our epoch is an **episode**. Our agent performs an *action* and receives updates or rewards from the environment until the state of the system is terminal. In our example, this means getting stuck in the maze.

The thing we are trying to learn is a policy. This policy is a function or a map of states to actions. It is a giant *n*-dimensional table of optimal actions given every possible state in our system.

Our ability to assess a state, S, is dependent on the assumption that it is a **Markov Decision Process** (**MDP**). As we've pointed out previously, this book is more concerned with implementation rather than theory; however, MDPs are fundamental to any real understanding of RL, so it's worth going over them in a bit of detail.

We use a capital S to denote all the possible states of our system. In the case of a maze, this is every possible location of an agent within the boundaries of the maze.

We use a lowercase s to denote a single state. The same applies to all actions, A, and an individual action, a.

Each pair (s, a) produces a distribution of the rewards, R. It also produces P, which is referred to as the transition probability, where for a given (s, a), the distribution of possible next states is $s(t + 1)$.

We also have a hyperparameter, which is the discount factor (*gamma*). In the vein of hyperparameters generally, this is something we set ourselves. This is the relative value assigned to the predicted reward for a given time step. For example, let's say we want to assign a greater value to the predicted rewards in the next time step, rather than after three time steps. We can represent this in the context of our objective in order to learn an optimal policy; the pseudocode looks like this:

OptimalPolicy = max(sum(gamma x reward) for timestep t

Breaking down the conceptual components of our DQN further, we can now talk about the value function. This function indicates the cumulative reward for a given state. For example, early on in our maze exploration, the cumulative expected reward is low. This is because of the number of possible actions or states our agent could take or occupy.

Q-learning

Now, we come to the real meat of our system: the Q-value function. This includes the cumulative expected reward for actions $a1$, $a2$, and a given state, s. We are, of course, interested in finding the optimal Q-value function. This means that not only do we have a given (s, a), but we have trainable parameters (the sum of the product) of the weights and biases in our DQN that we modify or update as we train our network. These parameters allow us to define an optimal policy, that is, a function to apply to any given states and actions available to the agent. This yields an optimal Q-value function, one that theoretically tells our agent what the best course of action is at any step. A bad football analogy might be the Q-value function as the coach yelling instructions into the rookie agent's ear.

So, when written in pseudocode, our quest for an optimal policy looks like this:

OptimalPolicy = (state, action, theta)

Here, *theta* refers to the trainable parameters of our DQN.

So, what is a DQN? Let's now examine the structure of our network in detail and, more importantly, how it is used. Here, we will bring in our Q-value functions and use our neural network to calculate the expected reward for a given state.

Like the networks we have covered so far, there are a number of hyperparameters we set upfront:

- Gamma (the discount factor of future rewards, for example, 0.95)
- Epsilon (exploration or exploitation, 1.0, skewed to exploration)
- Epsilon decay (the shift to the exploitation of learned knowledge over time, for example, 0.995)
- Epsilon decay minimum (for example, 0.01)
- Learning rate (this is still set by default despite using the **Adaptive Moment Estimation (Adam)**)
- State size
- Action size
- Batch size (in powers of two; start with 32 and tune your way from there)
- Number of episodes

We also need a fixed sequential memory for the experience replay feature, sizing it at 2,000 entries.

Optimization and network architecture

As for our optimization method, we use Adam. You may recall from Chapter 2, *What is a Neural Network and How Do I Train One?*, that the Adam solver belongs to the class of solvers that use a dynamic learning rate. In vanilla SGD, we fix the learning rate. Here, the learning rate is set per parameter, giving us more control in cases where sparsity of data (vectors) is a problem. Additionally, we use the root MSE propagation versus the previous gradient, understanding the rate of change in the shape of our optimization surface and, by doing so, improving how our network handles noise in the data.

Now, let's talk about the layers of our neural network. Our first two layers are standard feedforward networks with **Rectified Linear Unit** (ReLU) activation:

$$output = activation(dotp(input, weights) + bias)$$

The first is sized according to the state size (that is, a vector representation of all the possible states in the system).

Our output layer is restricted to the number of possible actions. These are achieved by applying a linear activation to our second hidden dimension's output.

Our loss function depends on the task and data we have; in general, we will use MSE or cross-entropy loss.

Remember, act, and replay!

Beyond the usual suspects involved in our neural network, we need to define additional functions for our agent's memory. The remember function takes a number of inputs, as follows:

- State
- Action
- Reward
- Next state
- Is done

It appends these values to the memory (that is, a sequentially ordered list).

We now define how an agent takes an action in an act function. This is where we manage the balance between the exploration of the state space and the exploitation of learned knowledge. These are the steps to follow:

1. It takes in one value, that is, the `state`.
2. From there, it applies `epsilon`; that is, if a random value between 0 and 1 is less than `epsilon`, then take a random action. Over time, our epsilon decays, reducing the randomness of the action!
3. We then feed the state into our model to make a prediction about what action to take.
4. From this function, we return `max(a)`.

The additional function we need is for the experience replay. The steps that this function take are as follows:

1. Create a random sample (of `batch_size`) selected from our 2,000-unit memory, which was defined and added to by the preceding remember function
2. Iterate over the `state`, `action`, `reward`, `next_state`, and `isdone` inputs, as follows:
    1. Set `target` = `reward`
    2. If not done, then use the following formula:

        Estimated future reward = current reward + (discounting factor (gamma) * call to model(predicted max expected reward) of next_state)

3. Map the future `reward` input to the model (that is, the predicted future `reward` input from the current state)
4. Finally, `replay` the memory by passing the current state and the targeted future reward for a single epoch of training
5. Decrement `epsilon` by using `epsilon_decay`

This covers the theory of DQNs and Q-learning more generally; now, it's time to write some code.

Solving a maze using a DQN in Gorgonia

Now, it's time to build our maze solver!

Using a DQN to solve a little ASCII maze is a bit like bringing a bulldozer to the beach to make sandcastles for your kids: it's completely unnecessary, but you get to play with a big machine. However, as a tool for learning about DQNs, mazes are invaluable. This is because the number of states or actions in the game is limited, and the representation of constraints is also simple (such as the *walls* of our maze that our agent cannot move through). This means that we can step through our program and easily inspect what our network is doing.

We will follow these steps:

1. Create a `maze.go` file for this bit of code
2. Import our libraries and set our data type
3. Define our `Maze{}`
4. Write a `NewMaze()` function to instantiate this `struct`

We also need to define our `Maze{}` helper functions. These include the following:

- `CanMoveTo()`: Check whether a move is valid
- `Move()`: Move our player to a co-ordinate in the maze
- `Value()`: Return the reward for a given action
- `Reset()`: Set player to start co-ordinates

Let's take a look at the start of the code for our maze generator. This is an excerpt, and the remainder of the code can be found in the book's GitHub repository:

```go
. . .
type Point struct{ X, Y int }
type Vector Point

type Maze struct {
    // some maze object
    *mazegen.Maze
    repr *tensor.Dense
    iter [][]tile
    values [][]float32

    player, start, goal Point

    // meta

    r *rand.Rand
}
. . .
```

Now that we've got the code that we need to generate and interact with a maze, we need to define the simple feedforward, fully connected network. This code should be familiar to us by now. Let's create nn.go:

```
...
type NN struct {
    g *ExprGraph
    x *Node
    y *Node
    l []FC

    pred *Node
    predVal Value
}

func NewNN(batchsize int) *NN {
    g := NewGraph()
    x := NewMatrix(g, of, WithShape(batchsize, 4), WithName("X"),
WithInit(Zeroes()))
    y := NewVector(g, of, WithShape(batchsize), WithName("Y"),
WithInit(Zeroes()))
    ...
```

We can now begin to define the DQN that will make use of this neural network. First, let's create a memory.go file with the basic struct type that captures information about a given episode:

```
package main

type Memory struct {
    State Point
    Action Vector
    Reward float32
    NextState Point
    NextMovables []Vector
    isDone bool
}
```

We will make a memory of []Memories and use it to store the per-play X/Y state coordinates, move vectors, expected reward, next states/possible moves, and whether the maze is solved.

Now we can edit our `main.go` and pull everything together. First, we define our possible moves across the *m x n* matrix that represents our maze:

```go
package main

import (
  "fmt"
  "log"
  "math/rand"
  "time"

  "gorgonia.org/gorgonia"
)

var cardinals = [4]Vector{
  Vector{0, 1},  // E
  Vector{1, 0},  // N
  Vector{-1, 0}, // S
  Vector{0, -1}, // W
}
```

Next, we need our main `DQN{}` structure to which we attach the neural network we defined earlier, our VM/Solver, and our DQN-specific hyper parameters. We also need an `init()` function to build the embedded feedforward network as well as the `DQN` object itself:

```go
type DQN struct {
  *NN
  gorgonia.VM
  gorgonia.Solver
  Memories []Memory // The Q-Table - stores
State/Action/Reward/NextState/NextMoves/IsDone - added to each train x
times per episode

  gamma float32
  epsilon float32
  epsDecayMin float32
  decay float32
}

func (m *DQN) init() {
  if _, err := m.NN.cons(); err != nil {
    panic(err)
  }
  m.VM = gorgonia.NewTapeMachine(m.NN.g)
  m.Solver = gorgonia.NewRMSPropSolver()
}
```

Next is our experience `replay()` function. Here, we first create batches of memory from which we retrain and update our network, gradually updating our epsilon:

```go
func (m *DQN) replay(batchsize int) error {
  var N int
  if batchsize < len(m.Memories) {
    N = batchsize
  } else {
    N = len(m.Memories)
  }
  Xs := make([]input, 0, N)
  Ys := make([]float32, 0, N)
  mems := make([]Memory, N)
  copy(mems, m.Memories)
  rand.Shuffle(len(mems), func(i, j int) {
    mems[i], mems[j] = mems[j], mems[i]
  })

  for b := 0; b < batchsize; b++ {
    mem := mems[b]

    var y float32
    if mem.isDone {
      y = mem.Reward
    } else {
      var nextRewards []float32
      for _, next := range mem.NextMovables {
        nextReward, err := m.predict(mem.NextState, next)
        if err != nil {
          return err
        }
        nextRewards = append(nextRewards, nextReward)
      }
      reward := max(nextRewards)
      y = mem.Reward + m.gamma*reward
    }
    Xs = append(Xs, input{mem.State, mem.Action})
    Ys = append(Ys, y)
    if err := m.VM.RunAll(); err != nil {
      return err
    }
    m.VM.Reset()
    if err := m.Solver.Step(m.model()); err != nil {
      return err
    }
    if m.epsilon > m.epsDecayMin {
      m.epsilon *= m.decay
    }
```

```
      }
      return nil
  }
```

The `predict()` function—called when we are determining the best possible move (or move with the greatest predicted reward)—is next. It takes a player's position in the maze and a single move, and returns our neural network's projected reward for that move:

```
func (m *DQN) predict(player Point, action Vector) (float32, error) {
  x := input{State: player, Action: action}
  m.Let1(x)
  if err := m.VM.RunAll(); err != nil {
    return 0, err
  }
  m.VM.Reset()
  retVal := m.predVal.Data().([]float32)[0]
  return retVal, nil
}
```

We then define our main training loop for n episodes, moving around the maze and building our DQN's memory:

```
func (m *DQN) train(mz *Maze) (err error) {
  var episodes = 20000
  var times = 1000
  var score float32

  for e := 0; e < episodes; e++ {
    for t := 0; t < times; t++ {
      if e%100 == 0 && t%999 == 1 {
        log.Printf("episode %d, %dst loop", e, t)
      }

      moves := getPossibleActions(mz)
      action := m.bestAction(mz, moves)
      reward, isDone := mz.Value(action)
      score = score + reward
      player := mz.player
      mz.Move(action)
      nextMoves := getPossibleActions(mz)
      mem := Memory{State: player, Action: action, Reward: reward,
NextState: mz.player, NextMovables: nextMoves, isDone: isDone}
      m.Memories = append(m.Memories, mem)
    }
  }
  return nil
}
```

We also need a `bestAction()` function that selects the best possible move to take, given a slice of options and an instance of our maze:

```go
func (m *DQN) bestAction(state *Maze, moves []Vector) (bestAction Vector) {
  var bestActions []Vector
  var maxActValue float32 = -100
  for _, a := range moves {
    actionValue, err := m.predict(state.player, a)
    if err != nil {
      // DO SOMETHING
    }
    if actionValue > maxActValue {
      maxActValue = actionValue
      bestActions = append(bestActions, a)
    } else if actionValue == maxActValue {
      bestActions = append(bestActions, a)
    }
  }
  // shuffle bestActions
  rand.Shuffle(len(bestActions), func(i, j int) {
    bestActions[i], bestActions[j] = bestActions[j], bestActions[i]
  })
  return bestActions[0]
}
```

Finally, we define a `getPossibleActions()` function to produce a slice of possible moves, given our maze and our little `max()` helper function for finding the maximum value in a slice of `float32`s:

```go
func getPossibleActions(m *Maze) (retVal []Vector) {
  for i := range cardinals {
    if m.CanMoveTo(m.player, cardinals[i]) {
      retVal = append(retVal, cardinals[i])
    }
  }
  return retVal
}

func max(a []float32) float32 {
  var m float32 = -999999999
  for i := range a {
    if a[i] > m {
      m = a[i]
    }
  }
  return m
}
```

With all those pieces in place, we can write our `main()` function to complete our DQN. We begin by setting `vars`, which includes our epsilon. Then, we initialize `DQN{}` and instantiate `Maze`:

We then kick off our training loop and, once complete, try to solve our maze:

```
func main() {
  // DQN vars

  // var times int = 1000
  var gamma float32 = 0.95 // discount factor
  var epsilon float32 = 1.0 // exploration/exploitation bias, set to
1.0/exploration by default
  var epsilonDecayMin float32 = 0.01
  var epsilonDecay float32 = 0.995

  rand.Seed(time.Now().UTC().UnixNano())
  dqn := &DQN{
    NN: NewNN(32),
    gamma: gamma,
    epsilon: epsilon,
    epsDecayMin: epsilonDecayMin,
    decay: epsilonDecay,
  }
  dqn.init()

  m := NewMaze(5, 10)
  fmt.Printf("%+#v", m.repr)
  fmt.Printf("%v %v\n", m.start, m.goal)

  fmt.Printf("%v\n", m.CanMoveTo(m.start, Vector{0, 1}))
  fmt.Printf("%v\n", m.CanMoveTo(m.start, Vector{1, 0}))
  fmt.Printf("%v\n", m.CanMoveTo(m.start, Vector{0, -1}))
  fmt.Printf("%v\n", m.CanMoveTo(m.start, Vector{-1, 0}))

  if err := dqn.train(m); err != nil {
    panic(err)
  }

  m.Reset()
  for {
    moves := getPossibleActions(m)
    best := dqn.bestAction(m, moves)
    reward, isDone := m.Value(best)
    log.Printf("\n%#v", m.repr)
    log.Printf("player at: %v best: %v", m.player, best)
    log.Printf("reward %v, done %v", reward, isDone)
    m.Move(best)
```

```
        }
    }
```

Now, let's execute our program and observe the outputs:

```
2019/06/17 22:29:33 width 21, height 11
Matrix (11, 21) [21 1]
[1 1 1 1 1 1 1 1 1 1 1 1 1 1 1 1 1 1 1 1 1]
[2 0 1 0 0 0 1 0 0 0 0 0 1 0 0 0 0 0 0 0 1]
[1 0 1 1 1 0 1 0 1 1 1 0 1 0 1 1 1 0 1 1 1]
[1 0 0 0 0 0 1 0 0 0 1 0 1 0 1 0 1 0 0 0 1]
[1 0 1 0 1 1 1 1 1 0 1 1 1 0 1 0 1 1 1 0 1]
[1 0 1 0 1 0 0 0 1 0 0 0 1 0 1 0 1 0 0 0 1]
[1 1 1 0 1 0 1 0 1 1 1 0 1 0 1 0 1 0 1 1 1]
[1 0 0 0 1 0 1 0 1 0 0 0 1 0 0 0 1 0 1 0 1]
[1 0 1 1 1 0 1 0 1 0 1 1 1 1 1 0 1 0 1 0 1]
[1 0 0 0 0 0 1 0 0 0 0 0 0 0 0 0 1 0 0 0 3]
[1 1 1 1 1 1 1 1 1 1 1 1 1 1 1 1 1 1 1 1 1]
{1 0} {9 20}
true
false
false
false
2019/06/17 22:29:33 episode 0, 1st loop
2019/06/17 22:29:44 episode 100, 1st loop
2019/06/17 22:29:55 episode 200, 1st loop
2019/06/17 22:30:07 episode 300, 1st loop
```

We can see the dimensions of the maze, as well as a simple representation of walls (1), a clear path (o), our player (2), and our maze exit (3). The next line, {1 0} {9 20}, tells us the exact *(X, Y)* co-ordinates of our player's starting point and the maze's exit, respectively. We then loop through the movement vectors as a sanity check and begin our training run across n episodes.

Our agent now moves through the maze:

```
2019/06/17 23:11:26 player at: {2 7} best: {1 0}
2019/06/17 23:11:26 reward -1, done false
2019/06/17 23:11:26
[1 0 1 1 1 1 1 1 1 1 1 1 1 1 1 1 1 1 1 1 1]
[0 0 1 0 0 0 1 0 0 0 0 0 1 0 0 0 0 0 0 0 1]
[1 0 1 1 1 0 1 0 1 1 1 0 1 0 1 1 1 0 1 1 1]
[1 0 0 0 0 0 1 0 0 0 1 0 1 0 1 0 0 0 0 1]
[1 0 1 0 1 1 1 1 1 0 1 1 1 0 1 0 1 1 1 0 1]
[1 0 1 0 1 0 0 0 1 0 0 0 1 0 1 0 1 0 0 0 1]
[1 1 1 0 1 0 1 0 1 1 1 0 1 0 1 0 1 0 1 1 1]
[1 0 0 4 1 0 1 0 1 0 0 0 1 0 0 0 1 0 1 0 1]
[1 0 1 1 1 0 1 0 1 0 1 1 1 1 1 0 1 0 1 0 1]
[1 0 0 0 0 0 1 0 0 0 0 0 0 0 0 0 1 0 0 0 3]
[1 1 1 1 1 1 1 1 1 1 1 1 1 1 1 1 1 1 1 1 1]
2019/06/17 23:11:26 player at: {3 7} best: {-1 0}
2019/06/17 23:11:26 reward 0, done false
```

You can experiment with different numbers of episodes (and episode lengths), and generate larger and more complex mazes!

Summary

In this chapter, we had look into the background of RL and what a DQN is, including the Q-learning algorithm. We have seen how DQNs offer a unique (relative to the other architectures that we've discussed so far) approach to solving problems. We are not supplying *output labels* in the traditional sense as with, say, our CNN from Chapter 5, *Next Word Prediction with Recurrent Neural Networks*, which processed CIFAR image data. Indeed, our output label was a cumulative reward for a given action relative to an environment's state, so you may now see that we have dynamically created output labels. But instead of them being an end goal for our network, these labels help a virtual agent make intelligent decisions within a discrete space of possibilities. We also looked into what types of predictions we can make around rewards or actions.

Now you can think about other possible applications for a DQN and, more generally, for problems where you have a simple reward of some kind but no labels for your data—the canonical example being an agent in some sort of environment. The *agent* and *environment* should be defined in the most general way possible, as you are not limited to a bit of math playing Atari games or trying to solve a maze. For example, a user of your website can be considered an agent, and an environment is a space in which you have some kind of feature-based representation of your content. You could use this approach to build a recommendation engine for news. You can refer to the *Further reading* section for a link to a paper that you may want to implement as an exercise.

In the next chapter, we will look into building a **Variational Autoencoder** (**VAE**) and learn about the advantages that a VAE has over a standard autoencoder.

Further reading

- *Playing Atari with Deep Reinforcement Learning*, available at https://www.cs. toronto.edu/~vmnih/docs/dqn.pdf
- *DRN: A Deep Reinforcement Learning Framework for News Recommendation*, available at http://www.personal.psu.edu/~gjz5038/paper/www2018_ reinforceRec/www2018_reinforceRec.pdf

8
Generative Models with Variational Autoencoders

In the previous chapter, we have looked into what DQN is and what types of predictions we can make around rewards or actions. In this chapter, we will look into how to build a VAE and about the advantages of a VAE over a standard autoencoder. We will also look into the effect of varying latent space dimensions on the network.

Let's take a look at another autoencoder. We've looked at autoencoders once before in Chapter 3, *Beyond Basic Neural Networks – Autoencoders and RBMs*, with a simple example, generating MNIST digits. Now we'll take a look at using it for a very different task—that is, generating new digits.

In this chapter, the following topics will be covered:

- Introduction to **variational autoencoders (VAEs)**
- Building a VAE on MNIST
- Assessing the results and changing the latent dimensions

Introduction to VAEs

A VAE is extremely similar in nature to the more basic autoencoder; it learns how to encode the data that it is fed into a simplified representation, and it is then able to recreate it on the other side based on that encoding. Unfortunately, standard autoencoders are usually limited to tasks such as denoising. Using standard autoencoders for generation is problematic, as the latent space in standard autoencoders does not lend itself to this purpose. The encodings they produce may not be continuous—they may cluster around very specific portions, and may be difficult to perform interpolation on.

However, as we want to build a more generative model, and we don't want to replicate the same image that we put in, we need variations on the input. If we attempt to do this with a standard autoencoder, there is a good chance that the end result will be rather absurd, especially if the input differs a fair amount from the training set.

The standard autoencoder structure looks a little like this:

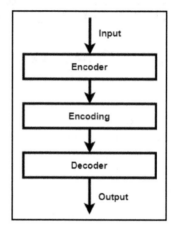

We've already built this standard autoencoder; however, a VAE has a slightly different way of encoding, which makes it look more like the following diagram:

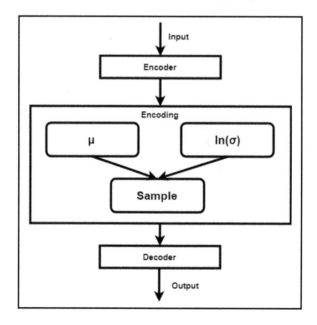

A VAE is different from the standard autoencoder; it has a continuous latent space by design, making it easier for us to do random sampling and interpolation. It does this by encoding its data into two vectors: one to store its estimate of means, and another to store its estimate of the standard deviation.

Using these mean and standard deviations, we then sample an encoding that we then pass onto the decoder. The decoder then works off the sampled encoding to generate a result. Because we are inserting an amount of random noise during sampling, the actual encoding will vary slightly every time.

By allowing this variation to occur, the decoder isn't limited to specific encodings; instead, it can function across a much larger area in the latent space, as it is exposed to not just variations in the data but to variations in the encoding as well, during the training process.

In order to ensure that the encodings are close to each other on the latent space, we include a measure called the **Kullback-Leibler** (**KL**) divergence into our loss function during training. KL divergence measures the difference between two probability functions. In this case, by minimizing this divergence, we can reward the model for having the encodings close by, and vice versa for when the model attempts to cheat by creating more distance between the encodings.

In VAEs, we measure KL divergence against the standard normal (which is a Gaussian distribution with a mean of 0 and a standard deviation of 1). We can calculate this using the following formula:

$$klLoss = 0.5 * sum(mean^2 + exp(sd) - (sd + 1))$$

Unfortunately, just using KL divergence is insufficient, as all we are doing is ensuring that the encodings are not spread too far apart; we still need to ensure that the encodings are meaningful, and not just mixed with one another. As such, for optimizing a VAE, we also add another loss function to compare the input with the output. This will cause the encodings for similar objects (or, in the case of MNIST, handwritten digits) to cluster closer together. This will enable the decoder to reconstruct the input better and allow us, via manipulation of the input, to produce different results along the continuous axis.

Building a VAE on MNIST

Being familiar with the MNIST dataset, as well as the results of a normal autoencoder, makes an excellent starting point for your future work. As you may recall, MNIST consists of many images of handwritten digits, each measuring 28 x 28 pixels.

Encoding

As this is an autoencoder, the first step is to build the encoding portion, which will look something like this:

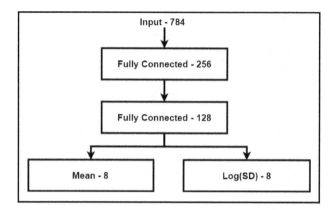

First, we have our two fully connected layers:

```
w0 := gorgonia.NewMatrix(g, dt, gorgonia.WithShape(784, 256),
gorgonia.WithName("w0"), gorgonia.WithInit(gorgonia.GlorotU(1.0)))

w1 := gorgonia.NewMatrix(g, dt, gorgonia.WithShape(256, 128),
gorgonia.WithName("w1"), gorgonia.WithInit(gorgonia.GlorotU(1.0)))
```

We give each layer a ReLU activation:

```
// Set first layer to be copy of input
l0 = x
log.Printf("l0 shape %v", l0.Shape())

// Encoding - Part 1
if c1, err = gorgonia.Mul(l0, m.w0); err != nil {
    return errors.Wrap(err, "Layer 1 Convolution failed")
}
if l1, err = gorgonia.Rectify(c1); err != nil {
     return errors.Wrap(err, "Layer 1 activation failed")
}
log.Printf("l1 shape %v", l1.Shape())

if c2, err = gorgonia.Mul(l1, m.w1); err != nil {
    return errors.Wrap(err, "Layer 1 Convolution failed")
}
if l2, err = gorgonia.Rectify(c2); err != nil {
     return errors.Wrap(err, "Layer 1 activation failed")
```

```
}
log.Printf("l2 shape %v", l2.Shape())
```

Then, we connect these to our mean and standard deviation layers:

```
estMean := gorgonia.NewMatrix(g, dt, gorgonia.WithShape(128, 8),
gorgonia.WithName("estMean"), gorgonia.WithInit(gorgonia.GlorotU(1.0)))

estSd := gorgonia.NewMatrix(g, dt, gorgonia.WithShape(128, 8),
gorgonia.WithName("estSd"), gorgonia.WithInit(gorgonia.GlorotU(1.0)))
```

These layers are used as they are, so they do not require a specific activation function:

```
if l3, err = gorgonia.Mul(l2, m.estMean); err != nil {
    return errors.Wrap(err, "Layer 3 Multiplication failed")
}
log.Printf("l3 shape %v", l3.Shape())

if l4, err = gorgonia.HadamardProd(m.floatHalf,
gorgonia.Must(gorgonia.Mul(l2, m.estSd))); err != nil {
    return errors.Wrap(err, "Layer 4 Multiplication failed")
}
log.Printf("l4 shape %v", l4.Shape())
```

Sampling

Now comes one part of the magic behind VAEs: sampling to create the encoding that we will feed into the decoder. For reference, we are building something a little like this:

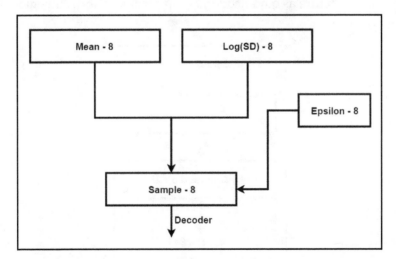

If you recall from earlier in the chapter, we need to add some noise during the sampling process, and we'll call this noise `epsilon`. This feeds into our sampled encoding; in Gorgonia, we can implement this with `GaussianRandomNode` with a mean of 0 and standard deviation of 1 as input parameters:

```
epsilon := gorgonia.GaussianRandomNode(g, dt, 0, 1, 100, 8)
```

We then feed this into our formula to create our sampled encoding:

```
if sz, err = gorgonia.Add(13,
gorgonia.Must(gorgonia.HadamardProd(gorgonia.Must(gorgonia.Exp(14)),
m.epsilon))); err != nil {
    return errors.Wrap(err, "Layer Sampling failed")
}
log.Printf("sz shape %v", sz.Shape())
```

The preceding code might be difficult to read. In simpler terms, what we are doing is the following:

```
sampled = mean + exp(sd) * epsilon
```

This gives us a sampled encoding using both the mean and standard deviation vectors plus a noise component. This ensures that the result is not quite the same every time.

Decoding

After we have got our sampled encoding, we then feed it to our decoder, which is essentially the same structure as our encoder, but in reverse. The arrangement looks a little like this:

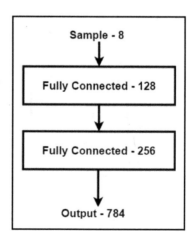

The actual implementation in Gorgonia looks like the following:

```
// Decoding - Part 3
if c5, err = gorgonia.Mul(sz, m.w5); err != nil {
    return errors.Wrap(err, "Layer 5 Convolution failed")
}
if l5, err = gorgonia.Rectify(c5); err != nil {
    return errors.Wrap(err, "Layer 5 activation failed")
}
log.Printf("l6 shape %v", l1.Shape())

if c6, err = gorgonia.Mul(l5, m.w6); err != nil {
    return errors.Wrap(err, "Layer 6 Convolution failed")
}
if l6, err = gorgonia.Rectify(c6); err != nil {
    return errors.Wrap(err, "Layer 6 activation failed")
}
log.Printf("l6 shape %v", l6.Shape())

if c7, err = gorgonia.Mul(l6, m.w7); err != nil {
    return errors.Wrap(err, "Layer 7 Convolution failed")
}
if l7, err = gorgonia.Sigmoid(c7); err != nil {
    return errors.Wrap(err, "Layer 7 activation failed")
}
log.Printf("l7 shape %v", l7.Shape())
```

We put a `Sigmoid` activation on the last layer, as we want the output to be more continuous than ReLU usually provides.

Loss or cost function

As discussed in the first part of the chapter, we optimize for two different sources of loss.

The first loss we optimize for is the actual difference between the input image and the output image; this is ideal for us if the difference is minimal. To do this, we expose the output layer and then calculate the difference to the input. For this example, we are using the sum of the squared errors between the input and output, nothing fancy. In pseudocode, this looks like the following:

```
valueLoss = sum(squared(input - output))
```

In Gorgonia, we can implement it as follows:

```
m.out = 17
valueLoss, err :=
gorgonia.Sum(gorgonia.Must(gorgonia.Square(gorgonia.Must(gorgonia.Sub(y,
m.out)))))
if err != nil {
    log.Fatal(err)
}
```

Our other loss component is the KL divergence measure, for which the pseudocode looks like the following:

```
klLoss = sum(mean^2 + exp(sd) - (sd + 1)) / 2
```

Our implementation in Gorgonia is more verbose, with a generous use of `Must`:

```
valueOne := gorgonia.NewScalar(g, dt, gorgonia.WithName("valueOne"))
valueTwo := gorgonia.NewScalar(g, dt, gorgonia.WithName("valueTwo"))
gorgonia.Let(valueOne, 1.0)
gorgonia.Let(valueTwo, 2.0)

ioutil.WriteFile("simple_graph_2.dot", []byte(g.ToDot()), 0644)
klLoss, err := gorgonia.Div(
    gorgonia.Must(gorgonia.Sum(
        gorgonia.Must(gorgonia.Sub(
            gorgonia.Must(gorgonia.Add(
                gorgonia.Must(gorgonia.Square(m.outMean)),
                gorgonia.Must(gorgonia.Exp(m.outVar)))),
            gorgonia.Must(gorgonia.Add(m.outVar, valueOne)))))),
    valueTwo)
if err != nil {
    log.Fatal(err)
}
```

Now, all that's left is a little bit of housekeeping and tying everything together. We will be using the Adam's `solver` for this example:

```
func (m *nn) learnables() gorgonia.Nodes {
    return gorgonia.Nodes{m.w0, m.w1, m.w5, m.w6, m.w7, m.estMean, m.estSd}
}

vm := gorgonia.NewTapeMachine(g,
gorgonia.BindDualValues(m.learnables()...))
solver := gorgonia.NewAdamSolver(gorgonia.WithBatchSize(float64(bs)),
gorgonia.WithLearnRate(0.01))
```

Let's now assess the results.

Assessing the results

You'll notice that the results of our VAE model are a fair bit fuzzier than our standard autoencoder:

Epoch	Standard Autoencoder	Variational Autoencoder
10		
20		
30		
40		
50		

In some cases, it also appears to be undecided between several different digits, like in the following example, where it appears to be getting close to decoding to a **7** instead of a **9**:

Epoch	Standard Autoencoder	Variational Autoencoder
10		
20		
30		
40		
50		

This is because we have specifically enforced the distributions to be close to each other. If we were to try to visualize this on a two-dimensional plot, it would look a little bit like the following:

You can see from this last example that it can generate several different variations of each of the handwritten digits, and also that there are certain areas in between the different digits where it appears to morph between several different digits.

Changing the latent dimensions

VAEs on MNIST typically perform reasonably well with two dimensions after enough epochs, but the best way to know this for certain is to test that assumption and try a few other sizes.

For the implementation described in this book, this is a fairly quick change:

```
w0 := gorgonia.NewMatrix(g, dt, gorgonia.WithShape(784, 256),
gorgonia.WithName("w0"), gorgonia.WithInit(gorgonia.GlorotU(1.0)))
w1 := gorgonia.NewMatrix(g, dt, gorgonia.WithShape(256, 128),
gorgonia.WithName("w1"), gorgonia.WithInit(gorgonia.GlorotU(1.0)))

w5 := gorgonia.NewMatrix(g, dt, gorgonia.WithShape(8, 128),
gorgonia.WithName("w5"), gorgonia.WithInit(gorgonia.GlorotU(1.0)))
w6 := gorgonia.NewMatrix(g, dt, gorgonia.WithShape(128, 256),
gorgonia.WithName("w6"), gorgonia.WithInit(gorgonia.GlorotU(1.0)))
w7 := gorgonia.NewMatrix(g, dt, gorgonia.WithShape(256, 784),
```

```
gorgonia.WithName("w7"), gorgonia.WithInit(gorgonia.GlorotU(1.0)))

estMean := gorgonia.NewMatrix(g, dt, gorgonia.WithShape(128, 8),
gorgonia.WithName("estMean"), gorgonia.WithInit(gorgonia.GlorotU(1.0)))
estSd := gorgonia.NewMatrix(g, dt, gorgonia.WithShape(128, 8),
gorgonia.WithName("estSd"), gorgonia.WithInit(gorgonia.GlorotU(1.0)))

floatHalf := gorgonia.NewScalar(g, dt, gorgonia.WithName("floatHalf"))
gorgonia.Let(floatHalf, 0.5)

epsilon := gorgonia.GaussianRandomNode(g, dt, 0, 1, 100, 8)
```

The basic implementation here is with eight dimensions; all we have to do to get it to work on two dimensions is to change all instances of 8 to 2, resulting in the following:

```
w0 := gorgonia.NewMatrix(g, dt, gorgonia.WithShape(784, 256),
gorgonia.WithName("w0"), gorgonia.WithInit(gorgonia.GlorotU(1.0)))
w1 := gorgonia.NewMatrix(g, dt, gorgonia.WithShape(256, 128),
gorgonia.WithName("w1"), gorgonia.WithInit(gorgonia.GlorotU(1.0)))

w5 := gorgonia.NewMatrix(g, dt, gorgonia.WithShape(2, 128),
gorgonia.WithName("w5"), gorgonia.WithInit(gorgonia.GlorotU(1.0)))
w6 := gorgonia.NewMatrix(g, dt, gorgonia.WithShape(128, 256),
gorgonia.WithName("w6"), gorgonia.WithInit(gorgonia.GlorotU(1.0)))
w7 := gorgonia.NewMatrix(g, dt, gorgonia.WithShape(256, 784),
gorgonia.WithName("w7"), gorgonia.WithInit(gorgonia.GlorotU(1.0)))

estMean := gorgonia.NewMatrix(g, dt, gorgonia.WithShape(128, 2),
gorgonia.WithName("estMean"), gorgonia.WithInit(gorgonia.GlorotU(1.0)))
estSd := gorgonia.NewMatrix(g, dt, gorgonia.WithShape(128, 2),
gorgonia.WithName("estSd"), gorgonia.WithInit(gorgonia.GlorotU(1.0)))

floatHalf := gorgonia.NewScalar(g, dt, gorgonia.WithName("floatHalf"))
gorgonia.Let(floatHalf, 0.5)

epsilon := gorgonia.GaussianRandomNode(g, dt, 0, 1, 100, 2)
```

Now all we have to do is recompile the code and then run it, which allows us to see what happens when we try a latent space with more dimensions.

As we can see, it's quite clear that **2 Dimensions** is at a disadvantage, but it isn't quite so clear as we move up the ladder. You can see that **20 Dimensions** produces appreciably sharper results on average, but really it looks like the **5 Dimension** version of the model may already be more than sufficient for most purposes:

Original	2 Dimensions	5 Dimensions	8 Dimensions	20 Dimensions
0	0	0	0	0
1	1	1	1	1
2	9	2	2	2
3	3	3	3	3
4	9	9	9	9
5	5	5	5	5
6	6	6	5	6
7	9	7	7	9
8	8	8	8	8
9	9	9	9	9

Summary

You have now learned how to build a VAE and about the advantages of using a VAE over a standard autoencoder. You have also learned about the effect of varying latent space dimensions on the network.

As an exercise, you should try training this model to work on the CIFAR-10 dataset and using convolutional layers instead of simple fully connected layers.

In the next chapter, we will look at what data pipelines are and why we use Pachyderm to build or manage them.

Further reading

- *Auto-Encoding Variational Bayes, Diederik P. Kingma,* and *Max Wlling*
- *Tutorial on Variational Autoencoders, Carl Doersh*
- *ELBO surgery: yet another way to carve up the variational evidence lower bound, Matthew D. Hoffman* and *Matthew J. Johnson*
- *Latent Alignment and Variational Attention, Yuntian Deng, Yoon Kim, Justin Chiu, Demi Guo,* and *Alexander M. Rush*

Section 3: Pipeline, Deployment, and Beyond!

This section is all about building deep learning pipelines, deployments, and all things to look forward to in the future of deep learning!

The following chapters are included in this section:

Building a Deep Learning Pipeline

9

So far, for the various deep learning architectures we've discussed, we have assumed that our input data is static. We have had fixed sets of movie reviews, images, or text to process.

In the real world, whether your organization or project includes data from self-driving cars, IoT sensors, security cameras, or customer-product usage, your data generally changes over time. Therefore, you need a way of integrating this new data so that you can update your models. The structure of the data may change too, and in the case of customer or audience data, there may be new transformations you need to apply to the data. Also, dimensions may be added or removed in order to test whether they impact the quality of your predictions, are no longer relevant, or fall foul of privacy legislation. What do we do in these scenarios?

This is where a tool such as Pachyderm is useful. We would like to know what data we have, where we have it, and how we can ensure that the data is feeding to our model.

We will now look into using the Pachyderm tool to handle dynamic input values in our networks. This will help us to prepare for the real-world use and deployment of our systems.

By the end of this chapter, you will have learned about the following:

- Exploring Pachyderm
- Integrating our CNN

Exploring Pachyderm

Our focus for this book is on developing deep learning systems in Go. So, naturally, now that we are talking about how to manage the data that we feed to our networks, let's take a look at a tool to do so that is also written in Go.

Pachyderm is a mature and scalable tool that offers containerized data pipelines. In these, everything you could possibly need, from data to tools, is held together in a single place where deployments can be maintained and managed and versioning for the data itself. The Pachyderm team sell their tool as **Git for data**, which is a useful analogy. Ideally, we want to version the entire pipeline so that we know which data was used to train, and which, in turn, gave us the specific prediction of X.

Pachyderm removes much of the complexity of managing these pipelines. Both Docker and Kubernetes run under the hood. We will explore each of these tools in greater detail in the next chapter, but for now, all we need to know is that they are critical for enabling reproducible builds, as well as scalable distributed training of our models.

Installing and configuring Pachyderm

A lot of excellent documentation for Pachyderm is available, and we won't attempt to rehash all of that here. Instead, we will take you through the basics and build a tutorial for managing a simple data pipeline to provide versioned image data to the CNN we built in Chapter 6, *Object Recognition with Convolutional Neural Networks*.

First, you need to install Docker Desktop and enable Kubernetes for your respective OS. For this example, we are using macOS.

Full instructions can be found at `https://docs.docker.com/docker-for-mac/install/`, but let's go over them in brief now:

1. Download the Docker `.dmg` file
2. Install or launch the file
3. Enable Kubernetes

To install and run Pachyderm, follow these steps:

1. To enable **Kubernetes**, select the appropriate checkbox after launching the Docker settings, as follows:

2. Ensure that you have a couple of green blobs indicating that your Docker and Kubernetes installations are running. If so, we can confirm that things look okay under the hood by dropping into a Terminal and running the following command:

```
# kubectl get all
NAME TYPE CLUSTER-IP EXTERNAL-IP PORT(S) AGE
service/kubernetes ClusterIP 10.96.0.1 <none> 443/TCP 7m
```

3. Before installing Pachyderm itself, ensure that the cluster is running. We are using Homebrew to install Pachyderm by using the following command (please note that you will need to have the latest version of Xcode installed):

```
brew tap pachyderm/tap && brew install pachyderm/tap/pachctl@1.9
Updating Homebrew...
...
==> Tapping pachyderm/tap
Cloning into '/usr/local/Homebrew/Library/Taps/pachyderm/homebrew-
tap'...
remote: Enumerating objects: 13, done.
remote: Counting objects: 100% (13/13), done.
remote: Compressing objects: 100% (12/12), done.
remote: Total 13 (delta 7), reused 2 (delta 0), pack-reused 0
Unpacking objects: 100% (13/13), done.
```

```
Tapped 7 formulae (47 files, 34.6KB).
==> Installing pachctl@1.9 from pachyderm/tap
...
==> Downloading
https://github.com/pachyderm/pachyderm/releases/download/v1.9.0rc2/
pachctl_1.9.0rc2_d
==> Downloading from
https://github-production-release-asset-2e65be.s3.amazonaws.com/236
53453/0d686a0
################################################################
##### 100.0%
/usr/local/Cellar/pachctl@1.9/v1.9.0rc2: 3 files, 62.0MB, built in
26 seconds
```

4. You should now be able to launch the Pachyderm command-line tool. First, check that the tool has been installed successfully by running the following command and observing the output:

```
pachctl help
Access the Pachyderm API.
..
Usage:
  pachctl [command]

Administration Commands:
  ..
```

5. We are almost done setting up our cluster so that we can focus on getting and storing data. The last thing to do is deploy Pachyderm on Kubernetes with the following command:

```
pachctl deploy local
no config detected at %q. Generating new config...
/Users/xxx/.pachyderm/config.json
No UserID present in config. Generating new UserID and updating
config at /Users/xxx/.pachyderm/config.json
serviceaccount "pachyderm" created
clusterrole.rbac.authorization.k8s.io "pachyderm" created
clusterrolebinding.rbac.authorization.k8s.io "pachyderm" created
deployment.apps "etcd" created
service "etcd" created
service "pachd" created
deployment.apps "pachd" created
service "dash" created
deployment.apps "dash" created
secret "pachyderm-storage-secret" created

Pachyderm is launching. Check its status with "kubectl get all"
```

> Once launched, access the dashboard by running "pachctl port-forward"

6. Execute the following command to check the status of your cluster. If you run the command just after deploying, you should see the containers being created:

```
kubectl get all
NAME READY STATUS RESTARTS AGE
pod/dash-8786f7984-tb5k9 0/2 ContainerCreating 0 8s
pod/etcd-b4d789754-x675p 0/1 ContainerCreating 0 9s
pod/pachd-fbbd6855b-jcf6c 0/1 ContainerCreating 0 9s
```

7. They then transition to `Running`:

```
kubectl get all
NAME READY STATUS RESTARTS AGE
pod/dash-8786f7984-tb5k9 2/2 Running 0 2m
pod/etcd-b4d789754-x675p 1/1 Running 0 2m
pod/pachd-fbbd6855b-jcf6c 1/1 Running 0 2m
```

The following section looks at how the data will be prepared.

Getting data into Pachyderm

Let's prepare our data. In this case, we are using the CIFAR-10 dataset from `Chapter 6`, *Object Recognition with Convolutional Neural Networks*. If you need a refresher, pull the data from the source at the University of Toronto, like so:

```
wget https://www.cs.toronto.edu/~kriz/cifar-10-binary.tar.gz
...
cifar-10-binary.tar.gz 100%[===================================>] 162.17M
833KB/s in 2m 26s
```

Extract the data to a temporary directory, and create `repo` in Pachyderm:

```
# pachctl create repo data
# pachctl list repo
NAME CREATED SIZE (MASTER)
data 8 seconds ago 0B
bash-3.2$
```

Now that we've got a repository, let's fill it with our CIFAR-10 image data. First, let's create individual directories and break up the various CIFAR-10 files so that we can just dump an entire directory of files (from our data or training sets).

Now we can execute the following command and then confirm that the data has made it to `repo` successfully:

```
#pachctl put file -r data@master -f data/
#pachctl list repo
NAME CREATED SIZE (MASTER)
data 2 minutes ago 202.8MiB
```

We can drill down to details of the files that `repo` contains:

```
pachctl list file data@master
COMMIT NAME TYPE COMMITTED SIZE
b22db05d23324ede839718bec5ff219c /data dir 6 minutes ago 202.8MiB
```

Integrating our CNN

We will now take our CNN example from an earlier chapter and make some updates that are necessary to package and deploy the network using data supplied by Pachyderm.

Creating a Docker image of our CNN

Pachyderm data pipelines are dependent on prebaked Docker images. The internet is full of Docker tutorials, so we'll keep things simple here and discuss what we need to do to take advantage of the simple deployment steps for any Go application.

Let's take a look at our Dockerfile:

```
FROM golang:1.12

ADD main.go /main.go

ADD cifar/ /cifar/

RUN export GOPATH=$HOME/go && cd / && go get -d -v .
```

And that's it! We're simply fetching the Go 1.12 image from Docker Hub and dropping our CIFAR CNN into our build. The final piece of our Dockerfile is a command to set GOPATH and meet our dependencies (for example, installing Gorgonia).

Execute the following command to build the Docker image and observe the output: `docker build -t cifarcnn`:

```
Sending build context to Docker daemon 212.6MB
Step 1/4 : FROM golang:1.12
 ---> 9fe4cdc1f173
Step 2/4 : ADD main.go /main.go
 ---> Using cache
 ---> 5edf0df312f4
Step 3/4 : ADD cifar/ /cifar/
 ---> Using cache
 ---> 6928f37167a8
Step 4/4 : RUN export GOPATH=$HOME/go && cd / && go get -d -v .
 ---> Running in 7ff14ada5e7c
Fetching https://gorgonia.org/tensor?go-get=1
Parsing meta tags from https://gorgonia.org/tensor?go-get=1 (status code
200)
get "gorgonia.org/tensor": found meta tag
get.metaImport{Prefix:"gorgonia.org/tensor", VCS:"git",
RepoRoot:"https://github.com/gorgonia/tensor"} at
https://gorgonia.org/tensor?go-get=1


. . .


Fetching https://gorgonia.org/dawson?go-get=1
Parsing meta tags from https://gorgonia.org/dawson?go-get=1 (status code
200)
get "gorgonia.org/dawson": found meta tag
get.metaImport{Prefix:"gorgonia.org/dawson", VCS:"git",
RepoRoot:"https://github.com/gorgonia/dawson"} at
https://gorgonia.org/dawson?go-get=1
gorgonia.org/dawson (download)
Removing intermediate container 7ff14ada5e7c
 ---> 3def2cada165
Successfully built 3def2cada165
Successfully tagged cifar_cnn:latest
```

Our container is now ready to be referenced in the Pachyderm data pipeline specification.

Updating our CNN to save the model

We need to add a simple function to our CNN example to ensure the model that gets produced is saved, so it can be managed as an object by Pachyderm. Let's add the following to `main.go`:

```go
func (m *convnet) savemodel() (err error) {
  learnables := m.learnables()
  var f io.WriteCloser
  if f, err = os.OpenFile("model.bin", os.O_CREATE|os.O_TRUNC|os.O_WRONLY,
0644); err != nil {
    return
  }
  defer f.Close()
  enc := json.NewEncoder(f)
  for _, l := range learnables {
    t := l.Value().(*tensor.Dense).Data() // []float32
    if err = enc.Encode(t); err != nil {
      return
    }
  }

  return nil
}
```

Creating a data pipeline

Now we need to specify a data pipeline in standard JSON. Here, we are mapping a repository to a directory and executing our network in either training or inference mode.

Let's look at our `cifar_cnn.json` file:

```json
{
 "pipeline": {
   "name": "cifarcnn"
 },
 "transform": {
   "image": "cifarcnn:latest",
   "cmd": [
 "go run main.go"
   ]
 },
 "enable_stats": true,
 "parallelism_spec": {
   "constant": "1"
 },
```

```
  "input": {
    "pfs": {
      "repo": "data",
      "glob": "/"
    }
  }
}
```

The options we've chosen here are straightforward, and you can see the references to the Docker image, commands, and switches, as well as `repo` and the mount point we're specifying. One thing to note is the `parallelism_spec` option. Setting this above the default of 1 allows us to scale a specific pipeline stage as required; for example, during the inference phase.

We can now create the pipeline from the preceding template:

```
pachctl create pipeline -f cifar_cnn.json
```

This returns you to Command Prompt if there is no error. You can then check the status of the pipeline:

```
pachctl list pipeline
NAME INPUT CREATED STATE / LAST JOB
cifarcnn data:/ 8 seconds ago running / running
```

We can change the level of *parallelism* dynamically and push the configuration out to our cluster by updating our template:

```
"parallelism_spec": {
   "constant": "5"
 },
```

Then, we can update our cluster and check the status of our job and the k8s cluster pods:

```
#pachctl update pipeline -f cifar_cnn.json
#pachctl list job
ID PIPELINE STARTED DURATION RESTART PROGRESS DL UL STATE
9339d8d712d945d58322a5ac649d9239 cifarcnn 7 seconds ago - 0 0 + 0 / 1 0B 0B
running

#kubectl get pods
NAME READY STATUS RESTARTS AGE
dash-5c54745d97-gs4j2 2/2 Running 2 29d
etcd-b4d789754-x675p 1/1 Running 1 35d
pachd-fbbd6855b-jcf6c 1/1 Running 1 35d
pipeline-cifarcnn-v1-bwfrq 2/2 Running 0 2m
```

After giving it some time to run (and using `pachctl logs` to inspect progress), we can see our successful job:

```
#pachctl list job
ID OUTPUT COMMIT STARTED DURATION RESTART PROGRESS DL UL STATE
9339d8d712d945d58322a5ac649d9239 cifarcnn 2 minutes ago About a minute 0 1
+ 0 / 1 4.444KiB 49.86KiB success
```

Interchangeable models

The flexibility of Pachyderm pipelines allows you to easily swap out one model for another with a simple update or push of the JSON pipeline we used previously.

What's the point in specifying a pipeline in JSON? It's to make it repeatable! Pipelines reprocess data (in our case, to make new predictions about the classes of labels) each time their data is updated.

Here, we update the `image` flag in `cifa_cnn.json` to refer to a version of our containerized CNN that, for whatever reason, does not contain dropout:

```
"image": "pachyderm/cifar_cnn_train:nodropout"
```

We can then update the pipeline on the cluster, like so:

```
pachctl update pipeline -f cifar_cnn.json --reprocesses
```

Mapping predictions to models

A great feature of Pachyderm—particularly for enterprise use cases—is the ability to version both your models and your predictions. Say you are predicting the chance a customer will repay a loan, and you see a batch of strange predictions. As part of troubleshooting why the model has made these decisions, if you are training multiple models across a large team, trawling through email chains and commit histories would be a bad idea!

So, work backward from the inference to the model, and simply run the following command:

```
#pachctl list job
```

You can then take the relevant commit hash and feed it to the following command, observing the details of the output:

```
#pachctl inspect job 9339d8d712d945d58322a5ac649d9239
...
Input:
{
  "pfs": {
    "name": "data",
    "repo": "data",
    "branch": "master",
    "commit": "b22db05d23324ede839718bec5ff219c",
    "glob": "/"
  }
}
...

#pachctl inspect commit data@b22db05d23324ede839718bec5ff219c
Commit: data@b22db05d23324ede839718bec5ff219c
Original Branch: master
Started: 11 minutes ago
Finished: 11 minutes ago
Size: 202.8MiB
```

You can see the exact commit of the model that was used to produce this prediction, the prediction's provenance, and in turn, the data that was used to train the model:

```
#pachctl list file data@adb293f8a4604ed7b081c1ff030c0480
COMMIT NAME TYPE COMMITTED SIZE
b22db05d23324ede839718bec5ff219c /data dir 11 minutes ago 202.8MiB
```

Using the Pachyderm dashboard

Technically, this is a feature of Pachyderm **Enterprise**, but since we want to be as inclusive as possible when it comes to the options you have, regardless of your use case, we're going to briefly cover the *dashboard* tool. Even if you have no need for an easy visual overview of your pipelines and data, 14-day trials are available for you to do some exploring of the feature set.

Launch `http://localhost:30800`. You will be presented with a basic screen that includes the following:

- Repositories (holding our CIFAR-10 data)
- Pipelines
- Jobs or logs
- Settings

Let's have a look at the following screenshot:

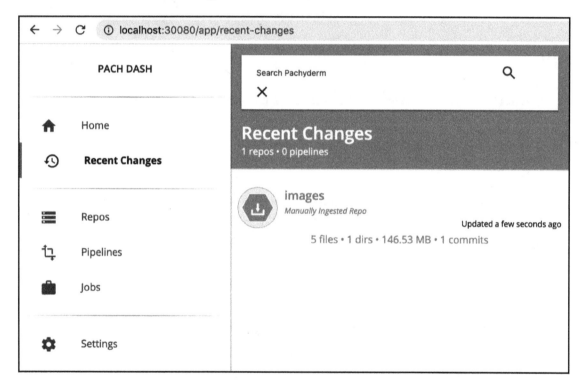

As you may recall, Pachyderm wants you to think of your data repositories as Git repositories. This is clearly visible when you drill down into the next screen:

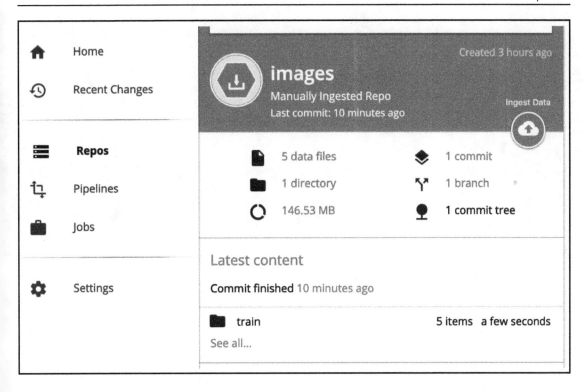

The dashboard offers a familiar GUI interface for the `pachctl` tool we've been using up until now.

Summary

In this chapter, we have gotten practical and looked at what is involved in starting the augmentation of input or output components of your model, and what tools we can use to do that in a maintainable and traceable way. At a high level, we learned about what a data pipeline is and why it is important, how to build/deploy/maintain pipelines in Pachyderm, and what tools to use to visualize our repositories and pipelines.

In the next chapter, we will look at a number of the technologies that sit underneath Pachyderm, including Docker and Kubernetes, and how we can use these tools to deploy stacks to the cloud infrastructure.

10
Scaling Deployment

Now that we've been introduced to a tool that manages data pipelines, it's time to peer completely under the hood. Our models ultimately run on the kinds of hardware we talked about in Chapter 5, *Next Word Prediction with Recurrent Neural Networks*, abstracted through many layers of software until we get to the point where we can use code such as `go build --tags=cuda`.

Our deployment of the image recognition pipeline built on top of Pachyderm was local. We did it in a way that was functionally identical to deploying it to cloud resources, without getting into the detail of what that would look like. This detail will now be our focus.

By the end of this chapter, you should be able to do the following:

- Identify and understand cloud resources, including those specific to our platform example (AWS)
- Know how to migrate your local deployment to the cloud
- Understand what Docker and Kubernetes are and how they work
- Understand the computation-versus-cost trade-off

Lost (and found) in the cloud

Having a beefy desktop machine with a GPU and an Ubuntu build is great for prototyping and research, but when it comes time to getting your model into production, and to actually making the day-to-day predictions required by your use case, you need compute resources that are highly available and scalable. What does that actually mean?

Imagine you've taken our **Convolutional Neural Network** (**CNN**) example, tweaked the model and trained it on your own data, and created a simple REST API frontend to call the model. You want to build a little business around providing clients with a service whereby they pay some money, get an API key, and can submit an image to an endpoint and get a reply stating what that image contains. Image recognition as a service! Does this sound good?

How would we make sure our service is always available and fast? After all, people are paying you good money, and even a small outage or dip in reliability could cause you to lose customers to one of your competitors. Traditionally, the solution was to buy a bunch of expensive *server-grade* hardware, usually a rack-mounted server with multiple power supplies and network interfaces to ensure service continuity in the case of hardware failure. You'd need to examine options for redundancy at every level, from disk or storage all the way through to the network and even internet connection.

The rule of thumb was that you needed two of everything, and this all came at a considerable, even prohibitive, cost. If you were a large, well-funded start-up, you had many options, but of course, as the funding curve dropped off, so did your options. It was inevitable that self-hosting became managed hosting (not always, but for most small or start-up use cases), which in turn became a standardized layer of compute stored in someone else's data center to the extent that you simply didn't need to care about the underlying hardware or infrastructure at all.

Of course, in reality, this is not always the case. A cloud provider such as AWS takes most of the boring, painful (but necessary) stuff, such as hardware replacements and general maintenance, out of the equation. You're not going to lose a disk or fall prey to a faulty network cable, and if you decide (*hey, this is all working well*) to serve 100,000 customers a day, then you can push a simple infrastructure spec change. No calls to a hosting provider, negotiating outages, or trips to the computer hardware store required.

This is an incredibly powerful idea; the literal nuts and bolts of your solution—the mix of silicon and gadgetry that your model will use to make predictions—can almost be treated as an afterthought, at least compared to a few short years ago. The skill set, or approach, that is generally required to maintain cloud infrastructure is called **DevOps**. This means that an individual has feet in two (or more!) camps. They understand what all these AWS resources are meant to represent (servers, switches, and load balancers), and how to write the code necessary to specify and manage them.

An evolving role is that of the *machine learning engineer*. This is the traditional DevOps skill set, but as more of the *Ops* side becomes automated or abstracted away, the individual can also focus on model training or deployment and, indeed, scaling. It is beneficial to have engineers involved in the entire stack. Understanding how parallelizable a model is, the kinds of memory requirements a particular model may have, and how to build the distributed infrastructure necessary to perform inference at scale all results in a model-serving infrastructure where the various design elements are not the product of domain specialization but rather an integrated whole.

Building deployment templates

We will now put together the various templates required to deploy and train our model at scale. These templates include:

- **AWS cloud formation templates**: Virtual instances and related resources
- **Kubernetes or KOPS configuration**: K8s cluster management
- **Docker templates or Makefile**: Create images to deploy on our K8s cluster

We are choosing a particular path here. AWS has services such as **Elastic Container Service (ECS)** and **Elastic Kubernetes Service (EKS)** that are accessible via simple API calls. Our purpose here is to engage with the nitty-gritty details, so that you can make informed choices about how to scale the deployment of your own use case. For now, you have greater control over container options and how processing is distributed, as well as how your model is called when deploying containers to a vanilla EC2 instance. These services are also expensive, as we'll see in a later section regarding cost and performance trade-offs when making these decisions.

High-level steps

Our mini CI/CD pipeline includes the following tasks:

1. Create or push training or inference Docker images to AWS ECS.
2. Create or deploy an AWS stack with Kubernetes cluster on an EC2 instance that allows us to do the next step.
3. Train a model or make some predictions!

We will now go through the details of each of these steps in turn.

Creating or pushing Docker images

Docker is certainly a tool that has attracted a lot of hype. The main reason for this, beyond human fashion, is that Docker simplifies things such as dependency management and model integration, allowing reproducible, widely deployable builds. We can define the things we need from an OS up front and parcel them all up at a point in time where we know the dependencies are fresh so that all our tweaking and troubleshooting will not be in vain.

We will need two things to create our image and get it to where we want it to go:

- **Dockerfile**: This defines our image, the version of Linux, the commands to run, and the default command to run when the container is launched
- **Makefile**: This creates the image and pushes it to AWS ECS

Let's first look at the Dockerfile:

```
FROM ubuntu:16.04

ARG DEBIAN_FRONTEND=noninteractive

RUN apt-get update && apt-get install -y --no-install-recommends \
        curl \
        git \
        pkg-config \
        rsync \
        awscli \
        wget \
        && \
    apt-get clean && \
    rm -rf /var/lib/apt/lists/*

RUN wget -nv
https://storage.googleapis.com/golang/go1.12.1.linux-amd64.tar.gz && \
        tar -C /usr/local -xzf go1.12.1.linux-amd64.tar.gz

ENV GOPATH /home/ubuntu/go

ENV GOROOT /usr/local/go

ENV PATH $PATH:$GOROOT/bin

RUN /usr/local/go/bin/go version && \
        echo $GOPATH && \
        echo $GOROOT
```

```
RUN git clone
https://github.com/PacktPublishing/Hands-On-Deep-Learning-with-Go

RUN go get -v gorgonia.org/gorgonia && \
        go get -v gorgonia.org/tensor && \
        go get -v gorgonia.org/dawson && \
        go get -v github.com/gogo/protobuf/gogoproto && \
        go get -v github.com/golang/protobuf/proto && \
        go get -v github.com/google/flatbuffers/go && \
        go get -v .

WORKDIR /

ADD staging/ /app

WORKDIR /app

CMD ["/bin/sh", "model_wrapper.sh"]
```

We can discern the general approach just by looking at the capitalized declarations at the start of each line:

1. Pick the base OS image with FROM.
2. Set boot with ARG.
3. Run a bunch of commands with RUN to get our Docker image into the desired state. Then ADD a directory of the staging data, mounted to /app.
4. Change to a new WORKDIR.
5. Execute the CMD command and our container will run.

We now need a Makefile. This file contains the commands that will build the images we just defined in our Dockerfile and push them to Amazon's container-hosting service, ECS.

This is our Makefile:

```
cpu-image:
                mkdir -p staging/
                cp model_wrapper.sh staging/
            docker build --no-cache -t "ACCOUNTID.dkr.ecr.ap-
southeast-2.amazonaws.com/$(MODEL_CONTAINER):$(VERSION_TAG)" .
                rm -rf staging/


cpu-push: cpu-image
            docker push "ACCOUNTID.dkr.ecr.ap-
southeast-2.amazonaws.com/$(MODEL_CONTAINER):$(VERSION_TAG)"
```

As with the other examples that we have already covered, we are using the `sp-southeast-2` region; however, feel free to specify your own. You will also need to include your own 12-digit AWS account ID.

From this directory (when the time comes, not just yet!) we can now create and push Docker images.

Preparing your AWS account

You will see a notification of API access to AWS in order for KOPS to manage your EC2 and related compute resources. The account associated with this API key will need the following IAM permissions too:

- **AmazonEC2FullAccess**
- **AmazonRoute53FullAccess**
- **AmazonS3FullAccess**
- **AmazonVPCFullAccess**

You can enable programmatic or API access by going into your AWS console and going through the following steps:

1. Click **IAM**
2. From the left-hand menu, select **Users** and then your user
3. Select **Security credentials**. You will then see the **Access Keys** section
4. Click **Create access key** and follow the instructions

The resulting key and key ID will be used in your `~/.aws/credentials` file or exported as a shell variable for use with KOPS and related deployment and cluster-management tools.

Creating or deploying a Kubernetes cluster

Our docker images have to run on something, so why not a collection of Kubernetes pods? This is where the magic of distributed cloud computing is apparent. Using a central data source, in our case AWS S3, many microinstances for either training or inference are spun up, maximizing AWS resource utilization, saving you money and giving you the stability and performance you need for enterprise-grade machine learning applications.

First, navigate to the /k8s/ directory in the repository that accompanies these chapters.

We will begin by creating the templates necessary to deploy a cluster. In our case, we are going to use a frontend for kubectl, the default Kubernetes command that interacts with the main API.

Kubernetes

Let's look at our k8s_cluster.yaml file:

```
apiVersion: kops/v1alpha2
kind: Cluster
metadata:
  creationTimestamp: 2018-05-01T12:11:24Z
  name: $NAME
spec:
  api:
    loadBalancer:
      type: Public
  authorization:
    rbac: {}
  channel: stable
  cloudProvider: aws
  configBase: $KOPS_STATE_STORE/$NAME
  etcdClusters:
  - etcdMembers:
    - instanceGroup: master-$ZONE
      name: b
    name: main
  - etcdMembers:
    - instanceGroup: master-$ZONE
      name: b
    name: events
  iam:
    allowContainerRegistry: true
    legacy: false
  kubernetesApiAccess:
  - 0.0.0.0/0
  kubernetesVersion: 1.9.3
  masterInternalName: api.internal.$NAME
  masterPublicName: api.hodlgo.$NAME
  networkCIDR: 172.20.0.0/16
  networking:
    kubenet: {}
  nonMasqueradeCIDR: 100.64.0.0/10
  sshAccess:
```

```
  - 0.0.0.0/0
subnets:
- cidr: 172.20.32.0/19
  name: $ZONE
  type: Public
  zone: $ZONE
topology:
  dns:
    type: Public
  masters: public
  nodes: public
```

Let's look at our `k8s_master.yaml` file:

```
apiVersion: kops/v1alpha2
kind: InstanceGroup
metadata:
  creationTimestamp: 2018-05-01T12:11:25Z
  labels:
    kops.k8s.io/cluster: $NAME
  name: master-$ZONE
spec:
  image: kope.io/k8s-1.8-debian-jessie-amd64-hvm-ebs-2018-02-08
  machineType: $MASTERTYPE
  maxSize: 1
  minSize: 1
  nodeLabels:
    kops.k8s.io/instancegroup: master-$ZONE
  role: Master
  subnets:
  - $ZONE
```

Let's look at our `k8s_nodes.yaml` file:

```
apiVersion: kops/v1alpha2
kind: InstanceGroup
metadata:
  creationTimestamp: 2018-05-01T12:11:25Z
  labels:
    kops.k8s.io/cluster: $NAME
  name: nodes-$ZONE
spec:
  image: kope.io/k8s-1.8-debian-jessie-amd64-hvm-ebs-2018-02-08
  machineType: $SLAVETYPE
  maxSize: $SLAVES
  minSize: $SLAVES
  nodeLabels:
    kops.k8s.io/instancegroup: nodes-$ZONE
```

```
  role: Node
  subnets:
  - $ZONE
```

These templates will be fed into Kubernetes in order to spin up our cluster. The tool we will use to deploy the cluster and associated AWS resources is *KOPS*. At the time of writing the current version of this tool is 1.12.1, and all deployments have been tested with this version; earlier versions may have compatibility issues.

First, we need to install KOPS. As with all our previous examples, these steps also apply to macOS. We use the Homebrew tool to manage dependencies and keep the installation localized and sane:

```
#brew install kops
==> Installing dependencies for kops: kubernetes-cli
==> Installing kops dependency: kubernetes-cli
==> Downloading
https://homebrew.bintray.com/bottles/kubernetes-cli-1.14.2.mojave.bottle.ta
r.gz
==> Downloading from
https://akamai.bintray.com/85/858eadf77396e1acd13ddcd2dd0309a5eb0b51d15da27
5b491
##################################################################
100.0%
==> Pouring kubernetes-cli-1.14.2.mojave.bottle.tar.gz
==> Installing kops
==> Downloading
https://homebrew.bintray.com/bottles/kops-1.12.1.mojave.bottle.tar.gz
==> Downloading from
https://akamai.bintray.com/86/862c5f6648646840c75172e2f9f701cb590b04df03c38
716b5
##################################################################
100.0%
==> Pouring kops-1.12.1.mojave.bottle.tar.gz
==> Caveats
Bash completion has been installed to:
  /usr/local/etc/bash_completion.d

zsh completions have been installed to:
  /usr/local/share/zsh/site-functions
==> Summary
  /usr/local/Cellar/kops/1.12.1: 5 files, 139.2MB
==> Caveats
==> kubernetes-cli
Bash completion has been installed to:
  /usr/local/etc/bash_completion.d
```

```
zsh completions have been installed to:
  /usr/local/share/zsh/site-functions
==> kops
Bash completion has been installed to:
  /usr/local/etc/bash_completion.d

zsh completions have been installed to:
  /usr/local/share/zsh/site-functions
```

We can see that KOPS has been installed, along with `kubectl`, which is the default K8s cluster-management tool that interacts directly with the API. Note that Homebrew often spits out warning-type messages regarding command completion, and it is safe to ignore these; however, if you get an error regarding the configuration of symlinks, follow the instructions to resolve conflicts with any existing local installation of `kubectl`.

Cluster management scripts

We also need to write a few scripts to allow us to set environment variables and spin up or bring down a Kubernetes cluster on demand. Here, we will bring together the templates we have written, KOPS or `kubectl`, and the AWS configuration we completed in previous sections.

Let's look at our `vars.sh` file:

```
#!/bin/bash


# AWS vars
export BUCKET_NAME="hodlgo-models"
export MASTERTYPE="m3.medium"
export SLAVETYPE="t2.medium"
export SLAVES="2"
export ZONE="ap-southeast-2b"

# K8s vars
export NAME="hodlgo.k8s.local"
export KOPS_STATE_STORE="s3://hodlgo-cluster"
export PROJECT="hodlgo"
export CLUSTER_NAME=$PROJECT


# Docker vars
export VERSION_TAG="0.1"
export MODEL_CONTAINER="hodlgo-model"
```

We can see here that the main variables are the container names, the K8s cluster details, and a bunch of specs for the kinds of AWS resources we want to spin up (and the zone to place them in). You will need to replace these values with your own.

Now we can make a corresponding script to unset the variables in our shell, an important part of cleaning up after we're done deploying or managing K8s clusters.

Let's look at our `unsetvars.sh` file:

```bash
#!/bin/bash

# Unset them vars

unset BUCKET_NAME
unset MASTERTYPE
unset SLAVETYPE
unset SLAVES
unset ZONE

unset NAME
unset KOPS_STATE_STORE

unset PROJECT
unset CLUSTER_NAME

unset VERSION_TAG
unset MODEL_CONTAINER
```

The script to bring up our cluster will now use these variables to determine what to call the cluster, how many nodes it has, and where it should be deployed. You will see that we use a little trick to pass environment variables into our Kubernetes templates or KOPS in a single line; in future versions, this may not be necessary, but it is a serviceable workaround for now.

Let's look at our `cluster-up.sh` file:

```bash
#!/bin/bash

## Bring up the cluster with kops

set -e

echo "Bringing up Kubernetes cluster"
echo "Using Cluster Name: ${CLUSTER_NAME}"
echo "Number of Nodes: ${SLAVES}"
echo "Using Zone: ${ZONE}"
echo "Bucket name: ${BUCKET_NAME}"
```

```
export PARALLELISM="$((4 * ${SLAVES}))"

# Includes ugly workaround because kops is unable to take stdin as input to
create -f, unlike kubectl
cat k8s_cluster.yaml | envsubst > k8s_cluster-edit.yaml && kops create -f
k8s_cluster-edit.yaml
cat k8s_master.yaml | envsubst > k8s_master-edit.yaml && kops create -f
k8s_master-edit.yaml
cat k8s_nodes.yaml | envsubst > k8s_nodes-edit.yaml && kops create -f
k8s_nodes-edit.yaml

kops create secret --name $NAME sshpublickey admin -i ~/.ssh/id_rsa.pub
kops update cluster $NAME --yes

echo ""
echo "Cluster $NAME created!"
echo ""

# Cleanup from workaround
rm k8s_cluster-edit.yaml
rm k8s_master-edit.yaml
rm k8s_nodes-edit.yaml
```

The corresponding down script will kill our cluster and ensure that any AWS resources are cleaned up accordingly.

Let's look at our cluster-down.sh file:

```
#!/bin/bash

## Kill the cluster with kops

set -e

echo "Deleting cluster $NAME"
kops delete cluster $NAME --yes
```

Building and pushing Docker containers

Now that we've done the hard work of preparing all our templates and scripts, we can get on with actually making the Docker images and pushing them to ECR ahead of a full cluster deployment.

First, we export the AWS credentials we generated earlier in this chapter:

```
export AWS_DEFAULT_REGION=ap-southeast-2
export AWS_ACCESS_KEY_ID="<your key here>"
export AWS_SECRET_ACCESS_KEY="<your secret here>"
```

Then we get the container repository login. This is necessary to allow us to push the created Docker image to ECR, which in turn will be pulled down by our Kubernetes nodes at model training or inference time. Note that this step assumes you have AWS CLI installed:

```
aws ecr get-login --no-include-email
```

The output of this command should resemble the following:

```
docker login -u AWS -p xxxxx
https://ACCOUNTID.dkr.ecr.ap-southeast-2.amazonaws.com
```

We can then execute `make cifarcnn-image` and `make cifarcnn-push` This will build the docker image we specified in the Dockerfile and push it to AWS's container storage service.

Running a model on a K8s cluster

You can now edit the `vars.sh` file we created earlier and set the appropriate values using your favorite command-line text editor. You will also need to create the bucket where k8s stores cluster information.

Once you have done this, you can bring up your Kubernetes cluster:

```
source vars.sh
./cluster-up.sh
```

KOPS is now interacting with Kubernetes via `kubectl` to spin up the AWS resources that will run your cluster and then configure K8s itself on these same resources. You will need to verify that your cluster has been brought up successfully before proceeding:

```
kops validate cluster
Validating cluster hodlgo.k8s.local

INSTANCE GROUPS
NAME ROLE MACHINETYPE MIN MAX SUBNETS
master-ap-southeast-2a Master c4.large 1 1 ap-southeast-2
nodes Node t2.medium 2 2 ap-southeast-2

NODE STATUS
```

```
NAME ROLE READY
ip-172-20-35-114.ec2.internal node True
ip-172-20-49-22.ec2.internal master True
ip-172-20-64-133.ec2.internal node True
```

Once all K8s masters return Ready, you can proceed with deploying your model across the cluster's nodes!

The script to do this is simple, and calls kubectl to apply the template in the same manner as our cluster_up.sh script.

Let's look at our deploy-model.sh file:

```
#!/bin/bash

# envsubst doesn't exist for OSX. needs to be brew-installed
# via gettext. Should probably warn the user about that.
command -v envsubst >/dev/null 2>&1 || {
  echo >&2 "envsubst is required and not found. Aborting"
  if [[ "$OSTYPE" == "darwin"* ]]; then
    echo >&2 "-----------------------------------------------"
    echo >&2 "If you're on OSX, you can install with brew via:"
    echo >&2 " brew install gettext"
    echo >&2 " brew link --force gettext"
  fi
  exit 1;
}

cat ${SCRIPT_DIR}/model.yaml | envsubst | kubectl apply -f -
```

Summary

Having now walked you through the under-the-hood details of how Kubernetes, Docker, and AWS can be used to throw as many resources at your model as your wallet will allow, there are a number of steps you can take to customize these examples to your use case or take your level of knowledge even further:

- Integrate this approach into your CI or CD tool (Bamboo, CircleCI, Puppet, and so on)
- Integrate Pachyderm into your Docker, Kubernetes, or AWS solution
- Experiment with the parameter server to do things such as distributed gradient descent and further optimize your model pipeline

Other Books You May Enjoy

If you enjoyed this book, you may be interested in these other books by Packt:

Deep Learning By Example

Ahmed Menshawy

ISBN: 978-1-78839-990-6

- Understand the fundamentals of deep learning and how it is different from machine learning
- Get familiarized with TensorFlow, one of the most popular libraries for advanced machine learning
- Increase the predictive power of your model using feature engineering
- Understand the basics of deep learning by solving a digit classification problem of MNIST
- Demonstrate face generation based on the CelebA database, a promising application of generative models

Deep Learning with PyTorch

Vishnu Subramanian

ISBN: 978-1-78862-433-6

- Use PyTorch for GPU-accelerated tensor computations
- Build custom datasets and data loaders for images and test the models using torchvision and torchtext
- Build an image classifier by implementing CNN architectures using PyTorch
- Build systems that do text classification and language modeling using RNN, LSTM, and GRU
- Learn advanced CNN architectures such as ResNet, Inception, Densenet, and learn how to use them for transfer learning

Leave a review - let other readers know what you think

Please share your thoughts on this book with others by leaving a review on the site that you bought it from. If you purchased the book from Amazon, please leave us an honest review on this book's Amazon page. This is vital so that other potential readers can see and use your unbiased opinion to make purchasing decisions, we can understand what our customers think about our products, and our authors can see your feedback on the title that they have worked with Packt to create. It will only take a few minutes of your time, but is valuable to other potential customers, our authors, and Packt. Thank you!

Index

CPSIA information can be obtained
at www.ICGtesting.com
Printed in the USA
FSHW022249090520
70005FS

9 781789 340990